CHARLES II'S ESCAPE FROM WORCESTER

CHARLES II's
ESCAPE FROM WORCESTER

A Collection of Narratives Assembled by Samuel Pepys

Edited by
WILLIAM MATTHEWS

UNIVERSITY OF CALIFORNIA PRESS   BERKELEY AND LOS ANGELES
1966

University of California Press
Berkeley and Los Angeles, California

© 1966 by The Regents of the University of California
Library of Congress Catalog Card Number: 66–26143
Designed by Marilyn Knudson
Printed in the United States of America

To
FRANKLIN D. MURPHY
Devoted Bibliophile
and
Chancellor Extraordinary

✒ Contents ✒

~Introduction~

With his defeat at the battle of Worcester, Charles II's career touched bottom. The invasion that he had hoped would restore him to the throne faltered before the reluctance of Englishmen to give armed aid to a Scottish-supported ruler, and at Worcester the King's Scottish forces proved unequal to the power of the Parliamentary army or Cromwell's military efficiency. As daylight retreated from the Worcestershire plain on Wednesday, September 3, 1651, Charles also took flight. For the next six weeks he was a fugitive in his own land, a price on his head, pursuers hard at his heels, holing up from Parliamentary hunters in the houses or cottages of one humble royalist after another, trying this line of escape and then that, until in the dark of October 16 he and Wilmot at length boarded the coal-grimed *Surprise* at Shoreham. Next day he was fast in the inhospitable safety of the continent, there to remain for nearly nine years before he was called back for the Restoration.

During the hazards of the weeks that followed Worcester, the young King showed at his best. Tall, big, swarthy, he was no beauty. Natural endowment and long training, however, had graced him with qualities that women, and men too, found hard to deny. His voice was deep and musical; an education in sports and his endowment of good health had made him athletic, slim, and graceful, a fine dancer, fencer, and rider. Physically courageous, nonchalant in danger, blessed with good humor, he also had an easy power to please. William Cavendish, Earl of Newcastle, his governor in boyhood, had guided him firmly toward a life of action. "Too much contemplation spoils action," the Earl instructed him, "and virtue consists in that. I confess I would rather have you study things than words, matter than language." He had also prepared the prince to make courtesy and civility the lodestars of his kingship. "The putting off of your hat and making a leg pleases more than reward or preservation. To women you cannot be too civil, especially to great ones. . . . Certainly, Sir, you cannot lose by courtesy."

Charles was only twenty-one when his cause disintegrated at Worcester; but his short life had been astonishingly full. His childhood had been spent in a world of piety, elegance, and ceremony, at Whitehall, Windsor, Hampton Court, Richmond, and Greenwich, directed insistently toward duties and attitudes proper to a kingship that his parents thought an appointment by God. Responsibility was loaded upon him even in childhood. At eight he was created Knight of the Garter; in the same year he was given a household to command.

His childhood world, described by his tutor John Earle and painted by Vandyke, was both pretty and pious. The world outside the royal palaces was less placid. Much of England was in revolt against social views that King and Queen considered beyond question. Reform and Liberty was becoming the cry of both Parliament and mob; society was becoming polarised into Cavaliers and Roundheads. Scarcely had the prince reached his teens than he was involved in civil war, first as a symbol and then as active participant. In his eleventh year he commanded his father's bodyguard at York. He was at Nottingham in 1642 when at the Garter celebration the royal celebration was raised and then blown down on an August evening. Two months later he soldiered at Edgehill when his hero, his dashing cousin Prince Rupert, led the famous charge that gave its false show of royal victory. In March, 1645, three months before his fifteenth birthday, Charles left Oxford to take nominal command of the King's western forces, in time for that sequence of royalist retreat and defeat which led to his first exile. In the night of March 2, 1646, he sailed from England, not to step again on his native soil until the invasion that ended in disaster at the battle of Worcester. The Scillies and Jersey, then St. Germain and The Hague were the scene of these drab years. Charles and his court of three hundred, councillors to barbers, behaved like all royal exiles: they were forever planning invasion to redeem their failed cause, forever begging money or men from any who sympathized —always to suffer the frustrations of plaintiffs whose friends offered little but words.

Charles had not seen his father since March 5, 1645, when they had bidden farewell in an Oxford rain. Since then the civil strife of Royalists and Roundheads had moved close to its tragic resolution. In 1648, the last Cavalier hope had been puffed out in the battle of Preston. For a long time the King lay prisoner in Carisbrooke Castle, and soon after Christmas, 1649, news came to The Hague of his coming trial by Parliament. Within a few days, Prince Charles sent his famous carte blanche, a paper bearing solely his signature, above which Parliament might insert whatever conditions it might demand for sparing the King's life. Each for his own reason, King and Cromwell both burned their copies. On January 30 the King went to the block and Parliament asserted its claims that supreme power lay in itself as representative of the People and that Charles I should be the last king of England.

When news of his father's execution reached the prince, wrote Edward Hyde, "he fell into all the confusion imaginable, sinking under the burden of his grief." Once restored, however, he came to grips with the problem of recovering the royal inheritance that Parliament denied. The Queen Mother urged him to become Catholic and to make his first step the winning of Ireland. Scotland proved more practical: it resolved to crown Charles as king and to help in avenging his father. Charles, after considerable havering, decided for a Scottish course. But he did so with no vast enthusiasm. The elders of the Presbyterian Kirk who dominated Scotland were scarcely *sympathique* to a prince whose casual amours had already begun; their demand that he renounce the Anglican faith for which his father had made himself martyr was hard to swallow. Charles tried evasion; but for all his shifts, the Scots were not to be denied. So Charles took the covenant, and thereupon set sail for Scotland with his poverty-stricken companions.

The year that followed was a schooling in Scottish piety. Charles was harassed by theologians, even in his bedroom; he was preached at without cease, about his own sins and those of his father, his mother, his companions, his soldiers; he was made to do penance; he was threatened with betrayal. With no little pride-swallowing, by the exercise of what diplomatic talents he had picked up from Newcastle and Hyde, somehow Charles managed to sidetrack the Kirk and to gather to his cause an almost united Scotland.

But the task had taken too long. Cromwell, once Ireland had been subdued, turned to Scotland. By the time Charles was ready, most of the Lowlands were in the Protector's hands and a strategy had been prepared for Charles's destruction. A way into England was deliberately left open, presenting the King with small choice but to advance down the route along which four royalist invasions have marched to destruction. Besides his own small company of Englishmen, Charles was supported by 20,000 Scotsmen—their general, Leslie. His hope was that as he moved down through Carlisle, Lancashire, and the Welsh marchlands, the loyal subjects of England would rise to his cause. At Stoke, a small reinforcement under the Earl of Derby did join with the Scots. Otherwise, Charles discovered that he had misjudged the English common man. English Presbyterians displayed small liking for the King's Catholic associates; English loyalists mani-fested no eagerness to serve with Scottish invaders or under a Scottish general. By the time he reached Worcester, in fact, Charles's army was smaller than it had been when he crossed the border.

Meanwhile, Cromwell was closing the bag. He himself followed through Yorkshire, gathering the English militia as he went. His cavalry was detailed to press the King's forces close, Harrison's troopers to lie on the flank, Lambert's on the rear. At Warrington they engaged the King in a delaying skirmish, thus permitting Cromwell to catch up and cut to the south. Joined by Fleetwood and the London contingent, Cromwell's forces, 30,000 men in all, then marched past Warwick to Stratford and Evesham, and so came to their destination before Worcester. That was on Thursday, August 28. On Friday, the King entered Worcester with Scots and English Royalists to a total of 16,000.

The engagement, delayed for a week, proved for four or five hours as stiff a battle as Cromwell had ever seen. The Scots lacked neither courage nor skill. But the odds were uneven.

Weary from their two-months march, heavily outnumbered, they were no real match for Cromwell's militia and New Model veterans. By the afternoon, Cromwell converted this his last battle into a royal rout. The Scots infantry surrendered or straggled away; the cavalry tried to cut a way through to the north, and most fell by the way. Charles fought to admiration; wrote one eyewitness:

> Certainly a braver prince never lived, having in the day of the fight hazarded his person much more than any officer of his army, riding from regiment to regiment, and leading them upon service with all the encouragement (calling every officer by his name) which the example and exhortation of a magnanimous general could afford, shewing so much steadiness of mind and undaunted courage, in such continual danger, that had not God covered his head and wonderfully preserved his sacred person, he must, in all human reason, needs have perished that day.

During twelve miles of wild ride to the north, several hundred runaways clung to the King's course. Convinced that these could be of no possible use, Charles, Derby, Buckingham, Wilmot, and some sixty gentlemen and officers slipped away to beyond Stourbridge. There they debated their courses in desperation. The King's own inclination was to race to London, hoping to get there before news came from Worcester. Derby proposed that the King take shelter nearby at Boscobel House, a recusant's place where he himself had been hidden a short time before. Persuaded by fatigue, Charles accepted Derby's proposal. And with that decision began the six weeks of desperate hide-and-seek that soon came to be known as the Royal Miracle.

The King's adventures during these weeks constitute the most stirring and romantic story in the chronicles of the English throne. It is scarcely surprising, therefore, that to the making of books about it there is seemingly no end. Pent up while Cromwell was in power, they gushed forth in flood when the King was restored to his throne. Thomas Blount's *Boscobel,* John Danvers' *The Royal Oake,* the anonymous *Monarchy Revived, The Five*

Faithful Brothers, An Exact Narrative and Relation, England's Triumph, and *White-Ladies* (the last a pirated edition of Blount's book) were all in the bookshops soon after the King's return in May, 1660. Swelling these records of the loyalties and seeming miracles that had preserved Charles from his Oliverian pursuers was a spate of broadside-ballads and other slighter treatments. All of these 1660 publications were journalistic products, stories and verses hurriedly basted up from general report and enquiries made of one or another of the many men and women who sheltered the King during the weeks of his flight.

After this initial rush, further versions continued to appear every now and again. Dr. G. Bate published in 1663 his *Elenchi motuum nuperorum in Anglia,* claiming that it recounted the King's own story.[1] Next year, A. Jenings's *Miraculum Basilicon* reprinted Bate's version, and supplemented it with the story of Charles's deliverance at Edgehill and in the Downs. In 1688 a Catholic pamphlet entitled *A Summary of Occurrences* retold the first part of the story from the personal testimony of Thomas Whitgreave and John Huddleston, who had both helped the King while he was in Shropshire.

Blount's *Boscobel,* the best of all these versions and the one that the King himself approved, was enlarged in 1662, and since then it has frequently been reprinted, once in twenty years on the average. The rest, save for Bate's book, which was reissued several times during the seventeenth and eighteenth centuries, seldom appeared again in print until nineteenth-century historians took to editing, separately and in collections, the original narratives of the royal escape.[2]

The participants who contributed to these versions were slow to compose their own independent stories. In 1667, Anne

[1] To judge from its errors and incompleteness, it is scarcely a direct version.

[2] The principal collections are these: John Hughes, *The Boscobel Tracts;* Allan Fea, *After Worcester Fight* and *The Flight of the King;* A. M. Broadley, *The Royal Miracle.* Among them, they reprint almost all the firsthand reports. The chief early secondhand reports appear in: Edward Hyde, Earl of Clarendon, *History of the Great Rebellion* (the documents from which he drew his account were published in *Clarendon State Papers* [Oxford, 1767]); Aurelian Cook, *Titus Britannicus;* Clement Walker, *The History of Independency;* Sir Philip Warwick, *Memoirs;* and Bulstrode Whitelocke, *Memorials of English Affairs.*

Wyndham, who had been one of the King's mainstays while he was hiding in Somerset, issued her story of that phase of the escape, giving it the title of *Claustrum Regale Reseratum*. This was reprinted in the 1680 and later editions of Blount's *Boscobel*. Colonel George Gounter, who made the arrangements for Charles's escape from Hampshire to Sussex and thence into France, had composed the story of the last ten days' adventures just before he died. Some twenty years after Gounter, in 1681, Robert Phillips set down detailed notes on his efforts to bring Charles from Somerset to some port in Hampshire or Sussex; and Thomas Whitgreave and Father John Huddleston recorded the adventures of the days when they combined to hide the King from his enemies in Shropshire. These are among the best-told as well as the most authentic narratives in the royal saga; but they did not get into print until the eighteenth or even the nineteenth-century.

The King himself never ceased to delight in regaling willing or even reluctant hearers with the story, and according to Sir Richard Browne he took almost immediate steps to get it into writing. Browne reported in 1681 that thirty years before, soon after Charles's arrival in Paris, the King had dictated to him his own story and that it had been sent to Théophraste Renaudot, the Parisian journalist, who had published an abstract of it as an *Extraordinaire* of the *Gazette de France* of 1651. But Browne's memory must have been confused: the only such item in the *Gazette* for 1651 or the following year is an account of the Battle of Worcester, and even that is not the King's own story.

So far as can now be determined, the earliest version of King Charles's own narrative to be set down on paper is the one that appears in Samuel Pepys's diary and was first published in Lord Braybrooke's edition of 1825. Pepys was a member of the excited company of courtiers and officials who, on May 11, 1660, set out for Holland to bring back the King for the Restoration. Twelve days later, the King proceeded in state from Breda to Scheveningen, boarded the *Naseby*, dined, and then changed the ship's name to *Royal Charles*. That done, the anchor was weighed and a course set for Dover. All the afternoon, Charles walked up and down the ship, very active and stirring, examining everything English on board. Then on the quarter-deck he fell to recounting the exciting tale of his escape. Samuel Pepys, who the day before had almost blown out his eye in his eagerness to be one of those who fired a gun in salute to the Monarch Restored, listened eagerly and emotionally to the miraculous tale. "It made me ready to weep," he wrote, "to hear the stories that he told of his difficulties that he had passed through." At that time, the diarist had no provision for recording the full story; but these are the matters that he remembered when he came to set down in the diary his annotations for that *dies mirabilis*, May 23, 1660:

> As his travelling four days and three nights on foot, every step up to his knees in dirt, with nothing but a green coat and a pair of country breeches on and a pair of country shoes that made him so sore all over his feet that he could scarce stir.
>
> Yet he was forced to run away from a miller and other company that took them for rogues.
>
> His sitting at table at one place, where the maister of the house, that had not seen him in eight years, did not know him but kept it private, when at the same table there was one that had been of his own *Regiment* at Worcester would not know him but made him drink the King's health and said that the King was at least four fingers higher than he.
>
> At another place he was by some servants of the house made to drink, that they might know him not to be a *Roundhead,* which they swore he was.
>
> In another place, at his *Inn,* the maister of the house, as the King was standing with his hands upon the back of a chair by the fire-side, he kneeled down and kissed his hand privately, saying that he would not ask him who he was but bid God bless him whether that he was going. Then the difficulty of getting a boat to get into France, where he was fain to plot with the maister thereof to keep his design from the four men and a boy (which was all his ship's company) and so got to *Feckham* in France.
>
> At Roane he looked so poorly that the people went into the rooms before he went away, to see whether he had not stole something or other.

When Pepys went into the great cabin in the evening, the company was even then still talking excitedly of the King's perils: "As, how he was fain to eat a piece of bread and cheese out of a poor boy's pocket. How at a *Catholique* house he was fain to lie in a *priests-hole* a good while in the house for his privacy." These notes agree in the main with the stories that were soon to appear in print, the differences being solely in details and coverage. But they represent only a few of the heads of the story that the King was later to set down, again with Pepys as his intermediary.

At the end of September, 1680, Charles went up to Newmarket, which he had by then popularized as a center for sporting amusements. Samuel Pepys, forty-seven and a sorely worried secretary to the Admiralty, went with him—mainly in hopes of getting his accounts settled and of obtaining payment of debts before it was too late. The time, as it proved, was much more momentous; for that was the occasion when, at the King's instigation, he set down Charles's full story of the weeks of peril that followed the defeat at Worcester. What prompted the King to withdraw himself from the delicious distraction of jockeys, horses, dogs, hawks, and ladies of pleasure is hard to guess; perhaps it was merely that at fifty, after nearly thirty years of telling the story orally, he realized that it was now high time to enshrine it in writing for the instruction and delight of the moody generations to come. Secretary Pepys, with his shorthand and his well-known efficiency, might suddenly have struck him as an obvious means for doing the job with minimal wastage of royal energy. Whatever the reasons, the King displayed unwontedly self-sacrificing application. Two lengthy sessions were devoted to the task: three hours in the evening of Sunday the third of October, and a similar period on the next Tuesday morning. During the second session Pepys ran over what he had taken down on the Sunday and also made various changes and additions. Later he edited the shorthand, and then transcribed the whole and got one of his clerks to make a fair copy on large foolscap pages.

The product of this joint labor was a magnificent narrative, a classic among tales of escape. From its plunging beginning to its quiet and triumphant close, it never ceases to compel the reader's attention. Like almost all the other firsthand narratives, however, it was slow to be printed. Pepys's intention—and also the King's, as one may judge—was to publish the story as soon as it had been edited and completed. As happened so often with Pepys's literary projects, however, the task fell victim to his absorption in public affairs, the sheer abundance of his scholarly interests, and his nagging perfectionism. As a result, the short-hand notes and the transcription were bound up with other documents on the same matter, shelved in Pepys's library, and in due course of time came to the Bibliotheca Pepysiana at Magdalene College, where they are perpetually displayed. Nothing appeared in print until 1766, when Sir David Dalrymple published Pepys's transcription under the title, *An Account of the Preservation of King Charles after the Battle of Worcester*. Since then, Dalrymple's not altogether accurate text has frequently been reprinted, separately and in collections. In that form it is universally esteemed as "the best and most authentic account of the most romantic incident in the history of the English throne."

The achievement is not Charles's alone. On the literary side and the factual, some of the credit must be given to Samuel Pepys. Any student who has enjoyed the pleasure of following the great diarist's drafting and polishing of his endless correspondence and reports is familiar with his concern for exactness in facts and dignity in presentation. In his youth, Pepys had written romance; in narrative literature his taste leaned to writing that had some of the bounce of the speaking voice. Even in writing that treated of solemn affairs, he looked for vitality. This, for example, is his reaction to a literary production that he had commissioned himself: "So home to dinner and to discourse with my brother upon his translation of my Lord Bacon's *Faber Fortunae* which I gave him to do and he hath done it but meanly, I am not pleased with it at all—having done it only *literally*, but without any life at all."

Pepys's literary predilection for joining liveliness with formality explains much of the style of his transcription of the notes that he took down from the King's speaking. In the present edition, these shorthand notes have been transcribed anew in a punctilious way and set face to face with a correct text of Pepys's own transcription. From these the reader may see for himself that Pepys's transcription is not to be charged with the literalness that he objected to in his brother's translation of Bacon; by a multitude of small changes he gives life to the tale, greater accuracy, and elegance too.

To a modern and modest editor, there may seem a little *lèse-majesté* in this superior handling of the King's story. Pepys himself might not have wished to deny the charge. In moral and business affairs, he was not one of Charles's admirers; and he certainly had minimal regard for his talents as speaker or storyteller. In April, 1664, after he had heard the King address Parliament, his only comment was that ". . . he speaks the worst that ever I heard man in my life—worse then if he read it all, and he had it in writing in his hand." In January, 1667, after he had heard him recount stories of his experiences at the siege of Mardike and Dunkirk, his judgment was that although the stories themselves were pretty enough, yet "he tells them but meanly." For the superiority of his own verbal skills, the diarist could rely on public acclaim and his own self-assurance.

Pepys's shorthand notes are too brief to be a complete verbatim report; they must be his selection of what he considered most interesting in the King's story. The many changes that he made both on the shorthand and in his transcription reflect his notions of the proper way for the story to be told. The result is a classical success, and any critic who wishes to apportion credits for that triumph is in the position of one who is called on to judge the work of a first-rate journalist. Much of the story's effectiveness derives from the excitement of events and the memory and manner of the man who reported them; much of it lies also in the discrimination of the reporter and his skill in presenting the material is suitable form.

But Pepys was not simply a journalist, he was also a historian and a scholar. About the time that he took down these notes and recomposed them in longhand, John Evelyn was pleading with him to bolster the Royal Society, which was seemingly about to be dissolved. He was also replying to him about a wide range of historical studies: the early history of shipbuilding, the recent Dutch war, the battle of Lepanto, the privileges of the Cinque Ports, and Raleigh's notes on the defenses of England. Nor was John Evelyn the only virtuoso to be badgered for information, bibliographies, and documents. Of Dr. John Peachell, the old red-nosed friend who was now Master of Magdalene, for instance, the insatiable diarist demanded information on matters in the history of Egypt, ancient Britain, Parthia, and Greece.

As befitted an enthusiastic Baconian and a president of the Royal Society, Pepys maintained a most lively curiosity about physical experiments and current reports on the nature of Nature. Many of his own scholarly endeavors were thoroughly Baconian. The great collections of ship models, engravings, ballads, music, calligraphy, shorthand, and books and documents relating to war and the navy, which he assembled over many long years, were provision for meeting several of Bacon's demands in the *Essay on Projects* for particular histories of human activities and the natural conditions that motivated and shaped them: a history of music; a history of painting, sculpture, modelling, etc., (including collections of prints); a history of the printing of books, of writing, of sealing; a history of the art of war and the arts thereto belonging; a history of the art of navigation and of the crafts and arts thereto belonging.

For all his Baconianism, however, Pepys was primarily a scholar of pen and ink. His real bent was for history, and in this he was a historian of the new vogue, a man who gathered ancient documents like a lover but was not less delighted by the more living procedures of what we now call "oral history." For the latter, there is the witness of several of his special collections, and his response to hearing the Duke of York recount the story of Captain Allen's great sea victory over the Dutch: "I do purpose to get the whole relation if I live of Captain Allen himself." For the former, there is his reaction to Sir William Coventry's suggestion that he should write a history of the late Dutch War: ". . . it being a thing I much desire, and sorts mightily with my *genius.*" And to Coventry's offer to provide him with facilities for searching the documents: "I shall take great delight in doing of it." All of Pepys's many collections, in fact, represent his response to both Baconian research and the new historiography. Collection of basic materials was the new watchword in both fields, and it was Pepys's sheer zeal for collecting that as much as anything else prevented his ever bringing his materials into print.

In later years, in a period of forced unemployment, he did contrive to get some of his naval collection into publishable shape;

and it duly appeared as *Memoirs of the Navy* in 1690. For the rest, however, he seems to have reconciled himself to the role of good provider for other men's books. He set his library into logical order, catalogued it by author and subject, arranged for it to be ultimately housed in Magdalene College, and, probably to ensure that the name of the original collector of these research materials should not be forgotten when scholars came to use them, demanded that his arms should be stamped on all the books and also that the collection should be maintained forever as a distinct unit—the Bibliotheca Pepysiana, Samuel Pepys's library of books, engravings, and documents—without a single item added or a single one subtracted.

The present edition of Pepys's collection of documents relating to Charles II's escape is a fulfillment of the collector's own unfulfilled intention. Unlike his predecessors who had interviewed participants in that romantic episode, Samuel Pepys was in no wise content to whip his shorthand notes quickly into print. The first thing that occurred to him after he had transcribed them was to go on with the research that was needed to bring the King's document to perfection. Six months later, the Duke of York asked him for a transcript. In sending the copy, Pepys explained the grounds of his delay in publishing the story:

> My covetousness of rend'ring it as perfect, as the memory of any of the Survivers (interested in any part of that memorable Story) can enable me to make it, has ledde me into so many and distant enquirys relateing thereto, as have kept me out of a capacity of putting it together as I would, and it ought, and shall be, so soon as ever I can possess myselfe of all the Memorialls I am in expectacion of concerning it.

At that time he had already gathered in Colonel Robert Phillips' story. He was also awaiting Father John Huddleston's narrative and was seemingly on the way to getting a report from Thomas Whitgreave. Later in the same year he was on the track of the story that Sir Richard Browne declared the King had dictated to him in Paris in 1651, which Pepys understood—on incorrect information—was now in John Evelyn's possession. Instead, he

acquired an anonymous firsthand report on the Battle of Worcester and a copy of the warrant for Charles's arrest. Apart from some
notes he gathered during an interview with Father Huddleston,
in which he put questions similar to those that he had previously
put to the King to check the accuracy of the King's memory, this
was the sum of his collection by the end of 1681. In December,
1684, however, another set of documents came to him from
Gregory Alford, whom the King had once thought might give
him passage from Charmouth in Dorset. There Pepys closed his
collection of original records. Early in 1685 he added a copy of the
one 1660 print that was suitable for his collection—it was one of
the liveliest and it concentrated on those engaging workingmen,
the five Penderels—provided a table of contents for the whole
collection, and then had the collection bound. Scarcely had he
done so when he acquired a new manuscript, a copy of Colonel
George Gounter's narrative. This he inserted into his current
collection of miscellaneous documents, but for the future student's guidance he added a footnote on the matter to the table of
contents.[3]

The collection was not complete. The King's reputed first
account was still lacking, Whitgreave had not sent in his
narrative, there was no special report relating to events at Trent,
and Pepys had failed to achieve an interview with Phillips, which
he had intended. That may be why the collector failed the
expectations of his contributors, and simply committed the
incomplete collection to his library, where in due time it might
possibly be dealt with by later and less busy researchers.

Incomplete though it is, it is a splendid collection. If one
adds to it Whitgreave's story, which Pepys seems to have
instigated and tried to get, it contains all the best firsthand
narratives of the King's escape: Charles's own story, both in the
rough shorthand notes and in Pepys's more polished transcription,
and the liveliest of the tales that were told by people who helped
the King in his flight. We are too easily prone to take them all for
granted as admirable stories due solely to their authors. That

[3] A modernized copy of the manuscript was made *ca.* 1730 for Lord
Hardwicke, apparently by Thomas Astle: this is now British Museum
additional Manuscript 31955. Copies of Gounter's narrative and some other
items in Pepys's collection were made early in the eighteenth century by
Thomas Tanner, and went with his papers to the Bodleian Library.

attitude pays no proper credit to the collector. Had it not been for Samuel Pepys's known skill in shorthand and for his zeal as a historical researcher, few of these fine narratives might ever have been written.

The present edition of Pepys's collection may therefore be justified in several ways. It adds to the story of the King's escape by presenting some familiar accounts in their correct form and by providing some that have either not been printed or reprinted before. The edition provides the first public opportunity to appreciate the contribution Pepys made to the story that the King himself told. It also partly fulfills Pepys's original intent to publish his collection; and in so doing it displays one of his remarkable talents which would be very obvious were it not for the peerless brilliance of his diary—his originality and his skill as a historical researcher.

These are the considerations that have determined the form of this edition. The editing is deliberately modest. The historical sketch that begins this introduction is meant solely as a setting for such readers as may be unfamiliar with Charles II's youth. No attempt has been made to expatiate on historical topics that the documents suggest, even though some are tempting—the extent and locales of royalist opposition and the religious conflict that underlies Charles's adventures are but two examples. Such matters are left to a more ample occasion and to historians better qualified than the present editor, whose primary concern is with Samuel Pepys and the stories as stories. Annotation has also been kept to a minimum: to clarifications that Pepys himself might have ventured or a general reader might need; to notes on bibliographical matters, discrepancies between the various narratives, and details that show Pepys at work as collector and editor; and, lastly, to identifications of persons and places that appear in these tales. (For several reasons, these identifications have been placed in the index). To keep the Restoration flavor, the original spelling has been retained; but, to avoid irritation and for easier reading, capitalization and punctuation have been modernized in most of the documents and abbreviations have been filled out. In *An Exact Narrative*, however, the original capitals and punctuation have been retained, as essential elements in the style of that sometimes ecstatic tale. And in the two transcriptions from the shorthand of the King's dictated story, Pepys's and my own, the original detail is followed exactly. That procedure may not make for easy reading, but it is the only way to enable the interested student to discover how much of that classic story is due to Charles and how much to Samuel Pepys.

For the opportunity of publishing this edition, the editor owes several particular debts of gratitude. He now pays them in public: to the Master and Fellows of Magdalene College for their hospitality and their permission to publish; to Dr. John Ladborough and Derek Pepys Whiteley, the Pepysian librarians, for their help on every occasion of need; to the Research Committee at the University of California, Los Angeles, and Franklin Murphy, Chancellor of the same hive of learning, who have been most generous with the most practical of all forms of encouragement.

⫸A Synopsis of Events⫷

Wednesday, September 3. Charles II's army is defeated at Worcester. The King, dissuaded from hurrying to London, rides with his followers to Kniver Heath and agrees to Derby's proposal to shelter at Boscobel. Guided by Charles Giffard and Francis Yates, he then rides northward with Wilmot, Derby, and other gentlemen.[1]

Thursday, September 4. The King reaches White Ladies by three in the morning. The Penderel brothers reclothe him in country style, and he shelters in Spring Coppice, where Mrs. Yates brings him food. Wilmot goes to Huntbach's house at Brinsford.

At night, the King goes to Boscobel and thence goes with Richard Pendrell to Madeley, intending to cross the Severn into Wales. On the way they are alarmed by a miller at Evelin. The river is too strongly guarded, and they sleep that night in Francis Wolfe's barn at Madeley.

[1] The several reports sometimes differ by a day in their dating. The dating of this synopsis is one that seems to be logical and is supported by most of the documents. Hester W. Chapman's *The Tragedy of Charles II* (Boston, 1964) gives a somewhat different dating, which results from her belief that Clarendon, despite admitted errors, must have had good evidence for including some details that are absent from other reports, even though those details can be included only by adjusting dates. Her sequence is the same as that given in the present synopsis; but she has the King sleeping in a cottage on September 7 and returning to White Ladies next day, reaching Stratford and Long Marston on the 11th, Cirencester on the 12th, and Abbots Leigh on the 13th. She also has the King leaving Hambledon on October 14, Shoreham on the same day, and arriving at Fécamp on the 15th. Not only are these variant datings contrary to the majority of evidence, but some of them are also physically improbable.

Following a discussion between John Penderel, Father Huddleston, and Thomas Whitgreave, Wilmot goes at night to Whitgreave's at Moseley.

Friday, September 5. Abandoning the plan to escape through Wales, Charles returns to Boscobel.

Wilmot gets in touch with Colonel John Lane at Bentley Hall and begins arrangements for the King's departure southward. That night, Wilmot transfers to Bentley.

Saturday, September 6. The King had returned to Boscobel about daybreak; during the day he hides with Colonel Careless in an oak tree nearby. Richard Penderel learns in Wolverhampton that Whitgreave is willing to shelter the King at Moseley. That night, the King sups at Boscobel and sleeps in a hiding-place. During the day, Humphrey Penderel fobs off a parliamentary search party.

Sunday, September 7. The King spends the morning at Boscobel. In the afternoon, he sets out for Moseley with Careless. According to Clarendon, he was forced by blistered feet to refuge in a cottage, where he stayed overnight. Other versions have him going to Moseley and being welcomed by Whitgreave and Huddleston (in Clarendon they do so next day).

Monday, September 8. The King remains in a secret room at Moseley, while Huddleston's pupils (Preston, Paling, Reynolds) keep watch. Horses are brought from Colonel Lane's.

Tuesday, September 9. White Ladies is searched by parliamentary soldiers. Charles hides in his garret room at Moseley, watching soldiers on the Wolverhampton road and talking with Whitgreave. Whitgreave repels Southall, the priest catcher. About midnight, the King is taken to Bentley Hall.

Wednesday, September 10. At daybreak, the King leaves Bentley, riding before Mrs. Jane Lane in the guise of her servant "William Jackson." Their companions are Withy Petre (Mrs.

Lane's sister) and her husband, and a royalist officer named Henry Lascelles. Wilmot also leaves, to lodge with Sir Clement Fisher at Packington Hall.

On the road, the King chats with an anti-royalist blacksmith. At Wootton, he rides through a troop of enemy cavalry into Stratford-on-Avon. The Petres take leave, and Charles, Mrs. Lane, and Lascelles go on to Long Marston, where they stay the night with John Tomes.

Thursday, September 11. They continue through Chipping Campden, and put up for the night at Cirencester.

Friday, September 12. They proceed through Sodbury and Bristol, arriving by evening at George Norton's house at Abbots Leigh, three miles beyond Bristol.

The King stays there for the next three days. Attempts to get passage from Bristol fail. The King is recognized by Pope the butler, and almost recognized by a visitor. On the Monday, Mrs. Norton miscarries, and in the evening Wilmot arrives in the neighbourhood and is met by Pope.

Tuesday, September 16. The King decides to move on to Colonel Francis Wyndham's at Trent. In the morning he sets out with Mrs. Lane and Lascelles, and they lodge at Castle Cary. This day the Council of State issued an order for the King's apprehension.

Wednesday, September 17. The royal party reaches Trent in the evening, and are greeted by Wyndham and Wilmot.

During the next few days, Wyndham enquires of Giles Strangways at Lyme about passage from Weymouth, Lyme, or some Devonshire port, but none can be found. Wyndham then arranges at Lyme for William Ellesdon to hire a vessel to go to France.

Monday, September 22. Pretending to be with a runaway marriage party, the King rides toward Charmouth with Juliana Coningsby and others. They stay for some hours at Ellesdon's house in the hills, and then go on to Charmouth and stay all night at the inn, waiting for Captain Limbry to fetch them to the boat at Lyme. Limbry fails to show up. (Several explanations are given in different reports.)

Tuesday, September 23. No word coming from Limbry, the party moves on to Bridport to await word whether the ship would be ready this night. The King pushes into the inn through a crowd of soldiers. He is almost recognized by an ostler, but the party moves on before his suspicions can be confirmed. They are pursued, but slip off on a side road to Broad Windsor. They lodge at the inn, where forty soldiers are also lodged the same night.

Wednesday, September 24. The royal party returns to Trent in the evening. There the King remains until October 5, while attempts are made to secure transportation for him from some port in Hampshire or Sussex.

Wilmot goes to Salisbury and negotiates with several royalists (Phillips, Coventry, Horne, St. Barbe, Hewett) to get passage on a barque sailing from Southampton on the night of the 29th. The barque however is pressed into service by General Blake.

Phillips, Coventry, and Dr. Henchman decide to try the Sussex coast, and to get Colonel Gounter to help. They write to Gounter via Lawrence Hyde, and on Sunday October 5, Phillips goes to Trent to fetch the King.

Monday, October 6. Phillips guides the King, Mrs. Coningsby and Henry Peters to the widow Mary Hyde's at Heale House, five miles from Salisbury. They are welcomed by the widow and the King stays there in a hiding hole while his friends try to arrange for a boat. Widow Hyde recognized him as the King. For safety he goes to Stonehenge next day and examines the stones, returning to Heale House at night.

On the Tuesday, Wilmot visits Colonel Gounter at night and persuades him to help. The next day Gounter tries and fails to get a boat at Emsworth. He calls on his brother Thomas at Chichester, and on the 9th hears that his brother and William Rishton had had no luck. The Colonel then decides to try a French merchant, Francis Mancell, who makes arrangements for Captain Tattersall to carry the King and Wilmot from Shoreham to a port in Normandy. On Sunday, Phillip and Henchman go to Heale House to tell the King to be ready.

Monday, October 13. Wilmot and two Gounters, after hunting hares, meet the King and Phil and conduct them at sunset to the house of Thomas Symonds Hambledon, Hants. Symonds, the Gounters' brother-in-law, takes the King for a Roundhead, but welcomes them for the night.

Tuesday, October 14. The King, Phillips, and the Colonel travel to Brighton by way of Houton, Bramber, and Beeding; Wilmot follows and dissuades them from stopping at Beeding as the Colonel had arranged. The Colonel finds the George Inn at Brighton safe. The King and Wilmot arrive, and the landlord later recognizes the King. While the King and Wilmot sleep, the Colonel settles with Captain Tattersall.

Wednesday, October 15. Gounter wakes the King and Wilmot at two in the morning; they go to Shoreham and embark. The boat sets off at eight. The King arranges with Tattersall to hide his identity from the crew. Tattersall sails toward the Isle of Wight and then turns south.

Thursday, October 16. After a last-minute scare from a French sloop, they reach Fécamp and disembark at ten in the morning.
Next day they go on to Rouen, and after a day there they proceed to Paris and are met by the Queen Mother.

SAMUEL PEPYS'S
TABLE OF CONTENTS

The table of contents o Pepys's collection generally follows the order in which Pepys collected the documents, although this may not be true of the printed narative.

The added memorandum concerning Colonel Gounter's report is incorrect. The report is actually bound up in a Miscellaneous volume, where it commnces at page 183.

The table of contents is in a copyist's hand, apparently done from Pepys's own draft.

A. D. 1651.

A COLLECTION
of
PAPERS RELATING TO KING CHARLES THE SECOND'S ESCAPE FROM WORCESTER
Vizt.

Page

An original copy of an Order of the then Council of State for the discovery of Charles Stuard

The Account of his escape as dictated to Mr. Pepys by the King himselfe, October, 1680

1

MEMORANDUM. My having Coll. Gunter's Report
thereof in MSS, bound up in the 10th Volume of
my Consutilia, page 183.

─⌣II⌣─
RELATION FROM
THE QUEEN MOTHER

This *Relation* is concerned with the Battle of Worcester and not with the King's escape. The place that Pepys gave to it in the collection was dictated by the fact that it came to him after he had taken in shorthand the King's account of his flight. The order given to it in the present edition is determined by historical chronology and the desirability of beginning with the background of the King's escape.

The document was first published in a French translation in the *Gazette de France* for December, 1651, where it is said to have been written by a Scottish prisoner at Chester to another Scotsman in France. The earliest English publication was in Clarendon's *State Papers,* and thence in Hughes's *Boscobel Tracts* and various later collections of documents on Charles's flight. The Pepys text has not been published before. It must have been made from a copy essentially the same as Clarendon's. There are, however, many small differences of phraseology and word-order between the two texts, which may be attributed to copying changes made along either or both lines of transmission of the texts. They are recorded in the note appended to this document in the present edition.

The report is ordinarily known as "A Letter from a Prisoner at Chester," in accordance with the heading of the Clarendon text: "Copy of a letter from a Prisoner at Chester, the 17/27 of September and since reviewed and perfected by some on this side of the sea, who were in the fight." The phrase "this side of the sea" probably refers to France, to judge from the more specific headings and endorsements of the Pepys copy. These, although they are slightly contradictory, indicate that Sir Richard Browne, while he was the Resident in Paris in 1651, prepared the document for publication on the basis of letters and the oral testimony of the Queen Mother.

Pepys acquired the document, and his information about it, from John Evelyn, Browne's son-in-law. Some time in 1681, it would seem, he must have spoken with Evelyn about the report he had taken down from the King, and Evelyn apparently told him that he himself had an earlier firsthand report. This may be judged from a long letter that Evelyn wrote on December 6 of that year in reply to Pepys's queries about documents that Evelyn owned relating to naval and maritime history and to the rebellion of 1651. The last paragraph of this letter runs: "Lastly, *A Relation of his Majesty's Action and Escape at the fight at Worcester* when he came into France; which Sir Richard Br[owne] tells me he copied out of the then Queene Mother's letters. This was it which I believed he had taken from his Majesty's owne mouth, for 'tis long since I cast my eye upon it." The statement that the document was prepared for the press appears in an endorsement in the hand of the scribe who copied the table of contents of the Pepys collection.

The document is in a different hand from the rest and its pages are of different size. It is probably the very document that Evelyn sent, therefore. One of the endorsements is in a Pepysian hand; the second is in a third hand, which may be a scribe's or Evelyn's own.

> *This Relation was taken from her Majestie the Queene-Mother, who commanded Sir Rich: Browne (then his Majestie's Resident in Paris) to prepare it for the Presse.*[1]

Chester, 17 Sept. 1651

I believe you have too soone heard our misfortunes at Worcester, and it's possible there are amongst you that rather blame our proceedings then pitty us. But

---

[1] The endorsement of this document, in the same hand as that of the Contents-Page, runs: "A Relation of the King's Escape, as taken from the Queen Mother, 1651, by Sir Richard Browne, then Resident at Paris, and prepared for the Press." A further endorsement, possibly in John Evelyn's hand, runs: "Relation of his Majesties Escape at Worcester, taken by Sir R. Browne from Letters and the mouth of Queen Mother."

if they knew the state of our Masters affairs when he was in Schottland and here, they would say otherwise. It's most certain that Cromwell would not at any time be draw'n to hazard a battaile in Schottland, but upon such great advantages as were no way reasonable to be given, which induced his Majesty (finding Cromwell to have past the river Forth with most part of his forces, and engaged Northward towards St. Johnstons, thereby giving us the advantage of foure or five day's time) to put in execution that which indeed was originally his designe from the beginning of the campagne; namely, to march in person with his army into England, not doubting but this his generous enterprise would give great encouragement and opportunity to his friends to rise, and free themselv's from that yoke of tyrannie which lay so heavy on them.

Our army consisted of between ten and eleven [2] thousand horse and foote (with sixteen leather gunns) all absolutely under the command of his Majesty, who marched without any opposition untill he came to Appleby; where eleven or twelve troops of those horse which Harrison had left in England endeavoured to hinder our advancing, but were (without great difficulty) forced to retire: and so we went on (with what diligence might be, and without any impeachment) unto Warrington, where we found their army (consisting of about nine thousand men united under Lambert and Harrison) possessed of the bridge, which they had broken. From which the King, in the head of his first troops, did beat them, with losse to them and great hazard to his owne person. And (having made up the bridge with plankes) passed over his whole army, they retiring in such disorder, that besides their losse upon the retreat, at least three thousand of their men did that night disband. The King from thence continued his march to Worcester; they not daring to give him so much as one allarme all the way.

In Worcester, besides the garrison, his Majesty found five hundred horse, which Lambert had newly sent in; which presently, upon the approach of the army, quitted the place, leaving the Earle of Shrewsbury, and there diverse prisoners of note, which they had formerly taken. The citty was neither fortified nor victualled, onely an old broke wall, and a fort, in a

[2] Replacing "twelve."

manner slighted. His Majesties intention was not to have stay'd there, but to march on towards London; but the army was so wearied with their hasty and continued march of three and twenty dayes (whereof it rested onely one day at Penrith in Cumberland) that it was altogether impossible to advance, and no lesse necessary to [3] rest and refresh them.

After neare a weeks stay in Worcester (in which time his Majesty us'd all endeavours to get in Glocester, Hereford, and some other places; and likewise provided for the better arming and cloathing of his souldiers), Cromwell appeared with his army near Perry-wood (about a mile from Worcester); and having drawn his left wing towards the river of Severne, his Majesty sent out a party of a thousand commanded foot, and two hundred and fifty horse to have fallen upon them that night. But this designe was betrayed by ——— Gives, a townsman of Worcester (who was afterwards hanged), whereupon they drew of in the night to their body, leaving onely some guards which were beaten away. After this, Major-Generall Massy being sent to try his creditt about Glocester, and lying within a mile of Upton bridge, which was not so broken but that the enemy gott over upon a piece of timber (layd onely for the passage of foot-men); and for want of the placing of a sentinel, some of their foot got into the church of Upton. Whereupon Massy, having the alarme, came with some Horse, charged them, and beat them back over the river; and returning towards Upton, he found in the church those men who had possess'd themselves of it; who fired upon him, and there shott him thorough the left hand upon diverse places of his Armes, and killed his horse under him. After which he returned to Worcester with his brigade.

Upon Tuesday, September 12/2, toward night (which was the day before the fight), his Majesty had intelligence that fifteene hundred horse were gone to Bewdely and that a very strong party of horse and foot and canon were gone to Upton— which made his Majesty the next morning to call a councell of warre on the topp of the steeple at Worcester, whence the country round about might best be discovered, there to advise upon some action, whilest the enemy was thus divided and part of their forces gone farther off.

[3] Replacing "and."

The result of this consultation was to divide the army into two partys; the one to goe upon the one side of Perry wood and the other on the other, reserving a body to fall on and assist where need should require. Whilest this was going to be put in execution, his Majesty spied a body of the enemies foot, about a thousand, with carriages of poles and plankes and some canon, going towards the water-side (as was supposed, and proved afterwards true) with intention to make a bridge. Hereupon, his Majesty gave order to the Generall Officers to put the army in posture, and went himselfe in person out of the towne, where he found the parties already engaged neare Powicke, where the enemy were making two bridges to passe a part of their army over the rivers Severne and Teine, so as to gett to the other side of the towne of Worcester.

The King, leaving there two brigades of foot, making neare two thousand men, returned to put in execution his first designe of falling on the enemy at Perry wood; and accordingly, having ledd [4] out the army and ingaged it himselfe, charging in the head thereoff many severall times in person with great courage and successe returned towards Powick to command two brigades of foot to assist those who were already engaged upon that passe. After [5] which, his Majesty went again towards the maine body, which he already found disordered, and with some difficulty made them stand a while; butt [6] upon the enemies second firing, they were so dispersed that they rallied no more, but gave backe violently and forced the King to make into the towne.

The enemy, taking this advantage, fell close in with the reare of his Majesties horse; and at the same time, with their foot, seised upon the fort, so that our horse were able to stand no longer without the walls, and the King with much difficulty and danger gott into the towne at Sudbury gate about the shutting in of the evening. The enemies foot entred the towne before their horse, and our foot, in disorder, threw downe their armes. Whereupon the enemies foot fell to plunder. But the Kings horse, which were left in the towne, disputed it from street to street, and made great

[4] Replacing "in person."
[5] Replacing "but that also proved unsuccessfull."
[6] Replacing "and then."

slaughter of the enemy by reason of the greedinesse after pillage, in so much that the streets were full of dead bodies of horse and men; till at last, overmaistered with numbers, they were forced downe to the kay, where many rendred themselves prisoners. Onely Colonel Wogan about midnight broke thorough with fifty horse and marched after the King, who was some houres before gone out at St. Martins gate and marched Northward that night with a body of about six hundred horse in neare disorder thirty miles; where the next morning, finding the close pursuit of the enemy, and the country altogether unsecure, he consulted for his safety. And of his royall person, I can give no farther accompt. But certainly a braver prince never lived; having in the day of the fight hazarded his person much more then any officer of his army, riding from regiment to regiment, and leading them on upon service with all the encouragement (calling every officer by his name) which the example and exhortation of a magnanimous generall could afford, shewing so much steadinesse of mind and undaunted courage, in such continuall danger, that had not God covered his head and wonderfully preserved his sacred person, he must, in all humane reason, needs have perished that day.

Duke Hamilton was shott in the charge at Perry wood; where the King at the head of his owne regiment (that Duke accompanying him) brake thorough a regiment of foot, and forced backe a considerable body of the enemy's horse. The Duke, I heare, is since dead upon the cutting off of his leg at Worcester.

We hope God almighty will preserve his Majesties sacred person to be an instrument of his glory in the performance of great things hereafter, though it did not please the Divine Power at this time to give him the victory; which in all likelyhood he had obtained, had not the enemy so exceedingly overpowerd him in numbers, they being (as their owne party gave out) no lesse then three score thousand, whereas his Majesties army was not in all eleven [7] thousand fighting men, but so well governed as the like hath not been seene. For, in the whole march from Schottland to Worcester, they never tooke anything but what they paid for; and the discipline was so severe and so strictly observed, that diverse were shott to death onely for going out of their rankes to gather a

[7] Replacing "above fifteene."

few apples in an orchard as they marched, and another did undergoe the same punishment onely for taking a pint of beere without paying for it. It is a great comfort to us in this our calamity that his Majesty hath taken some private way (with onely the [8] Lord Wilmott) for his escape, for had he stayed with us, his person had inevitably fallen into the hands of the enemy.

On Thursday night (which was the day after the battaile) our Lieutenants-Generalls, Middleton and Lesley, left us, or lost us willingly; but were afterward taken and with Sir William Flemming brought prisoners hither. The Earle of Derby, Earle Lauderdale, Sir David Cunningham and Mr. Lane are prisoners here in the castle; and many others of quality are kept in private houses. They have already [9] condemned some, and what will become of us, I yet knowe nott.

VARIATIONS IN THE CLARENDON TEXT

NOTE: Most of Clarendon's variations are supported by the French translation in the *Gazette de France*.

page 26, l. 4, "on" for "upon." l. 23, "seven" for "nine"; l. 28, "retreating" for "retiring"; l. 35, "the night before" for "newly"; l. 39, "broken" for "broke."

page 27, l. 14, "at" for "that." l. 19, "lay" for "lying"; ll. 20–22, "but that the enemy's foot, for the want of placing a sentinel, got over upon a piece of timber (laid only for the convenience of foot passengers), after which a body of their horse did also pass the ford; some of their foot got into the church of Upton" for "but that the enemy . . . church of Upton"; l. 24 "their cavalry" for "them"; l. 25, "foot" for "men"; l. 26 "those" for "there".

page 28, l. 4, "while" for "whilest"; l. 5, "discovered" for "spied"; l. 7, "water's" for "water"; l. 8, "And immediately after, espying some fire given at the bridge of Powick, he gave order" for "Hereupon, his Majesty gave order"; l. 12, "bridge of boats" for "bridges"; l. 13 "the two" for "the"; l. 17, "accordingly" omitted; l. 30, "mount" for "fort."

[8] Replacing "the Duke of Buckingham." After "Wilmott" the words "and some few others of quality" are struck out.
[9] Replacing "condemned."

page 29, l. 8, "near" for "in neare"; l. 21, "in the first charge, which
    he performed with great honour" for "in the charge"; ll. 22–
    24, "in the head of those troops, broke through and forced
    back their horse to their body of foot" for "at the head.
    . . . enemy's horse."
page 30, l. 1, "passed" for "marched."

~(III)~

ORDER OF THE COUNCIL
OF STATE

This copy of the Order of the Council of State for the apprehension of Charles II was sent to Pepys by John Evelyn with his letter of December 6, 1681.

Tuesday, 16th of September, 1651
At the Councell of State at Whitehall

ORDERED:

That it be referred to the Committee of Examiners to use the best meanes they can for the discovery of Charles Stuart.
That it be referred to the Committee of Examiners to consider of the peticion of Lieut-Col. [   ] now prisoner in the Tower and to bayle him if they see cause.

Ex^r. Gualter Frost. Secretary

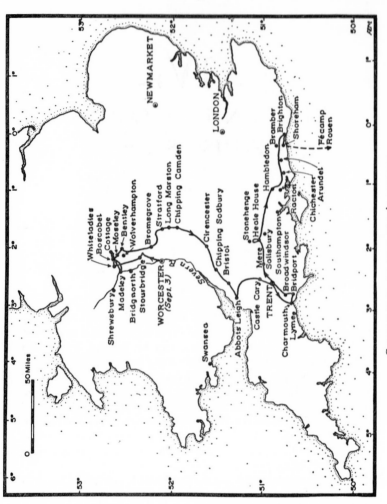

SKETCH-MAP OF THE KING'S FLIGHT

~IV~

THE KING'S ACCOUNT
OF HIS ESCAPE

The present document is the classic account of the King's escape, the one that the King dictated to Samuel Pepys at Newmarket in October, 1680, twenty-nine years after the events he narrates. It was first published eighty-six years after the dictating session at Newmarket as *An Account of the Preservation of King Charles II,* edited by David Dalrymple and printed for R. Sandby, 1766. This edition has been reprinted many times, separately and in collections of Boscobel documents, the latest being William Rees-Mogg's edition entitled *His Majesty Preserved* (London, 1954). All the editions I have examined follow Dalrymple's text, without check from the manuscript at Magdalene College.

Dalrymple's edition was the first scholarly publication based on Pepys's library, and it was appropriately initiated from Magdalene. The Master of the College, Dr. R. Sandby, D.D., brought the manuscript to Dalrymple's attention and gave him permission to publish it; and when it was published it was dedicated to Thomas Holles, Duke of Newcastle, then chancellor of the university. The edition is a simple one: a copy of Pepys's transcription, with a brief introduction and a few footnotes attributed to the King, Pepys, Huddleston, and Phillips. The text is substantially accurate, although Dalrymple modernized and regularized the language and filled lacunae (sometimes incorrectly); the notes, selected from other documents in Pepys's Boscobel collection, are occasionally attributed to the wrong persons. No indication is given that this is not the only document Pepys collected.

The text of Pepys's transcription which is printed in the present edition is taken from the manuscript, and the original notes that are strictly relevant to it are appended, as they are in the original. A second version, which is printed here face to face with Pepys's transcription, is the present editor's transcription from Pepys's short-hand notes, which follow his transcription in the collection. This new transcription has been made as exact as is possible in representing shorthand in print, including all changes that Pepys made. Words that Pepys wrote in longhand are given in italics; the strikeovers are the same; words Pepys inserted over the line are put into angle-brackets. The punctuation is unchanged, except that full stops have been used for Pepys's check marks. This punctiliousness is intended to facilitate study of what Pepys's own contribution to the narrative may have been, both on the shorthand version and in his transcription; but it also represents the tribute due to the basic document in the collection, the original form of the King's story. Text-variants are reported in footnotes; and, to avoid further complication of these pages, explana-tory notes are relegated to an appendix to the texts, these notes (pp. 80–84) referring to places marked by asterisks.

The endorsements to the shorthand notes indicate that Pepys took down the story at the King's instance while he was at Newmarket in the early days of October, 1680. For this purpose, he was with the King in his closet alone on two occasions: for three hours in the evening of Sunday, October 3, when he took down the first two-thirds of the story; and on Tuesday, October 5, in the morning, when the story was completed and notes were made on the first day's work.

Some significant deductions may be made from these facts and the form of the notes. The shapes of the shorthand are much cruder than those in the great diary, or even in the Tangier journal and the occasional letters that Pepys wrote in shorthand. Many symbols are overwritten in neater form—this seems to have been done when Pepys read over his notes. The roughness is patently the effect of hasty writing. Nevertheless, it is unlikely that the notes are completely verbatim. The first session of three hours is represented by about 6,000 words; the second by about 2,500 words, plus the King's answers to Pepys's questions on the first day's work. Even a slow stenographer might have been expected in this period of time to get down twice as much. Nor can the King have spoken at an average pace of thirty-five words a minute: only a carefully prepared story can be dictated so slowly, and that pace would not have resulted in the haste that is reflected in the shorthand. It would seem, therefore, that the notes may represent Pepys's selection from what the King said.

Stylistically the notes are uneven. Some have the rhythms and grammatical structures of speech, and they may well be the King's actual words. Many are more literary, as though they were composed for written rather than spoken communication. Some are almost disjointed from the general narrative and so telegraphic that they seem to be synopses of narrative sections, which may have been much longer in the actual telling. There are also sentences that begin with false starts or are grammatically incomplete. The numerous changes in the text may have various explanations. So far as can be judged from the notes, the King told his story in no clear-cut way; rather, he often changed tack, even in mid-sentence. Thus, the changes may have been made *en courant,* or in the second session, when the King corrected himself or refined a detail, or they may have been made when Pepys read over his notes preparatory to making his transcription. The latter can sometimes be distinguished by the fact that they simply complete a grammatical construction or provide a smoother reading for something that is already represented by the notes that are changed. The shorthand notes also show that Pepys's inclination during the interview was to record the narrative in third person form, but in revising them he changed his mind and altered the notes into the first person. The numerous additions inserted over the line or in blank spaces at the end of a paragraph must nearly all be Pepys's later additions. Some of them do not appear in his transcription. Several are simply aesthetic; most add small details of information. There are more of them in the first part of the narrative, so it is likely that a few were added as the result of Pepys's second session with the King. Some, however, are supplied from other sources, either to fill in names and details that the King did not remember or to supply a detail Pepys thought interesting.

Taken as a whole, the shorthand notes read like the jottings that a journalist makes in an important interview he means to put into print. In part they represent the informant's actual words; in part they employ a more summary form, which reports all important matters but also reduces details the reporter thinks unessential to the main story. Therefore, although they represent the King's own narrative, they represent it as Pepys would have it told in public—as somewhat more formal in grammar and vocabulary, as less diffuse and less rambling than the way in which the King may actually have told it, at some points more specific and accurate. This was achieved in the note form partly during the interview and partly in later editing. In the transcription, the process was carried much further. As we now have it, the transcription is a clerk's clean copy (there must have been another which Pepys sent to persons interested in his collection), and behind it there must have been a draft that was much closer to the shorthand notes and was later edited.

Except for a few accidentally omitted phrases, possibly the copyist's, the transcription is careful and respectful, in the sense that its matter and order do not differ from the notes. There are many differences, but almost all of them are linguistic and stylistic. The disjointed jottings and the rambling, colloquial structures of the shorthand are replaced by more formal and more logically ordered statements; many simple and compound sentences are transformed into periodic, balanced sentences like those Pepys used in his own public writing. Some gaps in the narrative are covered up; a few ambiguities are clarified; words that were repeated in close proximity are varied; adverbials are put closer to their verbs; some words and phrases are made more emphatic, and, to the same end, the order of clauses in a sentence is sometimes changed; grammatical lacunae are filled; a sentence is occasionally restated more economically; colloquial words are replaced by more formal ones; and some simple words give way to polysyllabic synonyms. Apart from a few gloss notes inserted into the text and the supplying of a name or two, the additions are few. The only significant change of order is that the detail about the soldiers in the streets of Bridport is transferred to a more logical position. The large effect of all these small changes is to make the narrative more literate and literary—more economical and logical in its language, more varied in its sentence patterns, more formal, and considerably more dignified in its tone.

Reckoning together the procedures that Pepys employed with the shorthand notes and the editing that he did in his transcription, it is not unfair to say that while the matter and its excitements are Charles's contribution, the selection and style that do much to make the document the minor classic that it is are in large measure the contribution of Samuel Pepys.

PEPYS'S TRANSCRIPTION

New Market
Sunday Octr. 3d and Tuesday Octobr. 5th 1680.
An Account of His Majesty's Escape from Worcester,
Dictated to Mr. Pepys, by the King himselfe.[1]

After that the Battell was so
absolutely lost as to be beyond hope of recovery, I began to
think of the best way of saveing myselfe: and the first thought
that came into my head was that (if I could possibly) I would get
to London, as soone (if not sooner) than the newes of our defeate
could gett there; and it being neere dark, I talked with some
(espetially with my Lord Rochester, who was then Willmott)
about their oppinions which would be the best way for me to
escape, it being impossible as I thought to get back into Scottland.
I found them mightily distracted and their opinions different of
the possibility of getting to Scottland, but not one agreeing with
mine for goeing to London, saveing my Lord Willmott; and the
trueth is, I did not impart my designe[2] of goeing to London to
any but my Lord Willmott. But we had such a number of beaten
men with us (of the Horse) that I strove as soone as ever it was
dark to gett from them. And though I could not gett them to
stand by me against the enemy, I could not gett ridd of them now
I had a minde to it.

Soe wee (that is my Lord Duke of Buckingham, Lauderdale, Derby, Willmot, Tom Blague, Duke Darcy and severall
others of my servants) * went along Northward towards Scottland: and at last we gott about 60 that were Gentlemen and
Officers and slipt away out of the High Roade that goes to
Lancastershire and kept to the right hand, letting all the beaten-
men goe along the greate roade, and ourselves not knowing very
well which way to goe, for it was then too late for us to gett to
London on Horse-Back rideing directly for it; nor could we doe it,
because there was yett many people of quallity with us that I
could not gett ridd of.

[1] The transcription by Pepys, title page.
[2] Replacing "minde."

Mr. Pepys's Original taken in Short-Hand.[1]

After[2] the battle was so absolutely lost ⟨as to be⟩ beyond hopes of ⟨recovery⟩ ~~a total defeat the king~~ ⟨I⟩ began to ~~try~~ think of the best way of saving ~~himself~~ myself and the first thought that came into ~~his~~ my head was that ⟨if ~~he~~ I could possibly⟩ ⟨I would⟩ get to London as soon if not sooner ~~as~~ then the news of ~~the~~ our defeat could get thither and it being near dark I talked with some ⟨especially with my Lord *Rochestr* who was then Wilmot⟩ ⟨about⟩ their opinions on which was the best way for me to escape. It being impossible as I thought to get into *Scotland*. But I found men ~~so~~ mightily distracted and their opinions ~~so~~ different of the possibility to get to *Scotland* that ~~though that he~~ ⟨I⟩ found none of ~~his~~ my opinion to go to London but my Lord *Willmot*. The truth is ~~the King~~ I did not report ~~his~~ my design of going to London ~~but to~~ ⟨to any but⟩ my Lord *Willmot*.

But we ~~were then in~~ ⟨had⟩ such a Number of beaten men with us ⟨of the Horse⟩ that I ~~strive~~ strove as soon as ever it was dark to get from them and though I could not ~~yet~~ get them to stand by me against the enemy I could not get rid of them ~~when~~ ⟨now⟩ I had a mind ⟨to it⟩.

So ~~we~~ we ⟨that is my Lord D of Buckingham Lauderdale Derby Wilmot Tom Blague ~~and~~ Duke Darcy and several ⟨others⟩ of my servants⟩ went along ~~from me~~ Northward towards *Scotland* and ~~were~~ at last we got about 60 that were gentlemen and officers [2] and slipped away out of the high common road that goes to Lancashire and ~~we~~ kept on the right hand ~~leaving~~ letting all the beaten men go along the ~~big~~ great road. We not knowing ~~how~~ very well ~~then~~ which ~~we~~ way to go. For it was then too late for us to get to *London* a horse back riding directly for it. And we could not too. Because there was yet ~~so~~ many people of quality with ~~him~~ us that ~~he~~ I could not get rid of ~~them.~~

[1] This heading has been added: the hand is the same as that of the Contents-Page.
[2] Written over "when."

Soe we rodd through a Towne,* short of Woolverhampton, between that and Worcester, and went through, there lyeing a Troope of the Enemyes there that Night. Wee rode very quietly through the Towne, they haveing no boddy to Watch, nor they suspecting us noe more then we did them. Which I learnt afterwards from a Country fellow. Wee went that night about 25 myles to a place called *White-Ladyes* hard by Tong-Castle, by the advice of Mr Giffard; where we stopt and gott some little refreshment of Bread and Cheese, such as we could gett, it being just begining to be day. This White-Ladyes was a private House that Mr. Giffard, who was a Staffordshire-Man had told me belonged to honest people that lived thereabouts.*

And just as we came theither, there came in a Country Fellow that told us there were 3000 of our Horse just hard by Tong-Castle upon the Heath, all in disorder under David Leshley and some other of the Generall Officers. Upon which, there was some People of quality that were with me who were very earnest that I should goe to him and endeavour to gett into Scottland. Which I thought was absolutely impossible, knowing very well that the Country would all rise upon us, and that men who had deserted me when they were in good Order would never Stand to me when they have been beaten.

This made me take the Resolucion of putting my selfe into a disguise, and endeavouring to gett a Foote to London in a Country-Fellowes habbit, with a pair of ordinary grey Cloath Britches, a Leathern Dublett and a greene Jerkin * which I tooke in the House of White-Ladyes. I also cutt my Haire very short, and flung my Cloathes into a Privy-House, that noe Boddy might see that any boddy had beene Stripping themselves, I acquainting none with my Resolucion of goeing to London but my Lord Willmott, they all desireing me not to acquaint them with what I intended to doe, because they knew not what they might be forced to confess: On which Consideracion they with one Voyce begged of me not to tell them what I intended to doe.

Soe all the Persons of Quallity and Officers who were with me (except my Lord Willmott, with whome a place was agreed upon for our meeting at London if we Escaped, and who endeavoured to goe on [3] Horse-backe, in regard as I think of his

[3] Replacing "to."

So we rid through a town   short of *Wol*verhampton ~~and brought~~ between that and *Worcestr* ~~and kept~~ went through the town where there was a troop of the enemies lay that night ~~we~~ we riding very quietly through the town and they having no body to watch we passed through they not suspecting us nor we them. Which ~~the king~~ ⟨I⟩ ~~knew~~ ⟨learnt⟩ afterwards by a country fellow.

~~They~~ ⟨we⟩ went that night about 25 mile to a place called White .Ladies hard by Tong Castle. And there we stop and got some little refreshment of ~~such~~ bread and cheese ⟨such⟩ as we could get. It being just beginning to be day (⟨this *Wh. Ladys* being⟩ a private house that Mr. *Gifford* who was a Stafford shire man had told ~~him~~ me was honest people that lived thereabouts) and just as we were there there came in a country fellow telling ~~me~~ us [3] that there was 3000 of our horse just by Tong Castle upon ~~health~~ heath all in disorder under *David Lesly* and some other of the general officers upon which there was some of the people of quality that were with me that were very earnest that I would go to him and endeavour to get into *Scotland* which I thought was absolutely impossible knowing very well that the country would all rise upon us and men that had desarted me ~~would~~ when they were in good order would never stand to me when they had been beaten.

This made me take the resolution of putting myself into disguise and endeavouring to get a-foot to London in a country fellow's habit. A pair of ordinary gray cloth breeches, a leather double[t] and a green jerkin ~~he took them there~~ ⟨which I took⟩ in the house at White Ladies. I ⟨also⟩ cut off my hair ⟨very short⟩ and flung my clothes into a privy house that no body might see that any body had stript themselfs. Acquainting no body with my resolution of going to London but my Lord ~~Rochester that is~~ *Willmott*. They all desiring me not to acquaint them what I intended to do. Because they did not know what they might be ~~threatened~~ forced to confess. ~~They~~ ⟨Therefore they⟩ all with one voice ~~begging~~ begged ⟨of me⟩ that I would not tell them what I [4] intended to do.

So all these persons of quality (except my Lord W and he did entend to get a-horseback, he being too big he thinks to go afoot. And we have given one another a place of meeting at being to bigg to goe on foote) were resolved to goe and joyne with the 3000 disordered Horse, thinking to gett away with them to Scottland. But as I did before beleive, they were not marched 6 Myles after they gott to them but they were all routed by a single Troop of Horse. Which showes that my opinion was not wrong in not sticking to men that had Run away.

As soone as I was disguised, I tooke with me a Country Fellow whose name was Richard Penderell, whome Mr. Giffard had undertaken to answere for, to be an honest man. He was a Romane Catholique, and I choose to trust them, because I knew they had hideing-holes for Preistes, that I thought I might make use of in case of neede.

I was noe sooner gone (being the next morning after the Battle and then Broad Day) out of the House, with this Country-Fellow, but being in a great Wood,* I Sett my selfe at the Edge of the Wood neere the highway that was there (the better to see who came after us, and whether they made any search after the Runnawayes); and I immeadiately saw a Troop of Horse comeing by, which I conceived to be the same Troope that beate our 3000 Horse. But it did not looke like a Troop of the Armyes, but of the Militia, for the Fellow before it did not look at all like a Soldier.*

In this Wood I stayed all day without meate or drinke,* and by greate good Fortune it rained all the time, which hindred them, as I beleive, from comeing (into the Wood) to search for men that might be fledd thether. And one thing is remarkeable enough, that those with whome I have since spoake, of them that joyned with the Horse upon the Heath, did say that it rained little or Nothing with them all the day, but onely in the Wood where I was; this contributeing to my safety.

As I was in the Wood, I talked with the fellow about goeing towards London; and asking him many questions about what Gentlemen he knew, I did not finde that he knew any men of quallity in the way towards London. And the trueth is my minde changed as I lay in the Wood, and I Resolved of another way of makeing my Escape. Which was, to gett over the Severne into Whales; and soe to gett either to Swansey, or some other of

London if we escaped.) and officers that were there ~~is~~ were resolved to go and join with these horse in disorder (the 3000 by), thinking to get away (with them) to Scotland. But as I did believe before. They did not go 6 mile (after they got to them) but they were all ~~p~~ routed by one single troop of horse. Which showed that my opinion was not wrong in not sticking to men that had run away.

As soon as I was disguised I took with me a country fellow whose name was *Rd. Penderell* whom Mr. *Gifford* had ~~answered~~ (undertaken to answer) for to be a honest man. He was a Roman Catholic and I chose to ~~get into~~ trust them because I knew they had hiding holes for priests that I thought I might make use of in case of need.

I was no sooner gone ~~out~~ (being the next morning after the battle) (it being then broad day) out of the house and in a great wood that was there (with this country fellow) but I set myself at the edge of the wood near the high way that was there ((the better) to see ~~better~~ who came after us. Whether they [5] whether they made any search after the runaways). ~~And~~ but immediately I saw coming (by) a troop of horse which I conceive were the same troop that beat all our 3000 horse. But it did not look like a troop of the army. But of the militia. For the fellow before it did not not ~~like~~ look at all like a soldier.[3]

In this ~~state~~ wood I stayed all day without meat or drink and by great good fortune it rained all day long. Which I do believe hindered them from coming into the wood to see after any men that were fled into the wood. And one thing is remarkable enough. That ~~they~~ those that I spoke with since (of them) that went with those horse upon the heath say that it rained little or nothing with them all the day but only in the wood where I was. This contributing to my safety.

As I was in the wood I talked with the fellow about going towards London and asking him many questions what gentlemen he knew, I did not ~~know~~ find that he ~~found~~ knew toward London any men of quality. The truth is my mind changed as I lay in the wood and I resolved of another way of [6] another way of making my escape which was to get over the Severn into *Wales* and so to get either to *Swansey* or some other of the sea towns that I knew

[3] Shorthand reads "soder."

the Sea-Townes, that I knew had commerce with France; to the end I might gett over that way, as being a Way that I thought none would Suspect my takeing; besides, that I remembered severall honest Gentlemen that were of my acquaintance in Whales.

Soe that night, as soone as twas dark, Richd. Penderell and I tooke our Journey on Foot towards the Severne, intending to pass over at a [4] Ferry half way between Bridgenorth and Shrewsbury. But as we were goeing in the Night, we came by a Mill where I heard some people talking (Memorandum, that I had gott some bread and Cheese the night before at one of the Penderells Houses, I not goeing in) and as wee conceived it was about 12 or 1 a-Clock at Night; and the Country-Fellow desired me not to answere if any Boddy should ask me any Questions, because I had not gott the Accent of the Country.

Just as we came to the Mill, we could see the Miller (as I beleive) sitting at the Mill-doore, he being in White Cloathes, it being a very dark night; He called out, Who goes there? upon which Richd. Penderell answered, Neighbours goeing home, or some such-like wordes. Whereupon the miller cryed out, If you be neighbours stand, or elce I will knock you downe. Upon which we beleiveing there was Company in the House, the fellow bad me follow him close, and he Run to a Gate [5] that went up a dirty-lane up a Hill; and opening the Gate, the Miller cryed out, Rogues, Rogues; and thereupon some men came out of the Mill after us, which I beleived was Soldiers. Soe we fell running, both of us, up the lane as long as we could Runn, it being very deep and very dirty; Till at last I badd him leap over a hedge and lye still to heare if any boddy followed us.* Which we did, and continued lyeing downe upon the Ground about halfe an hower; when hearing noe body come, we continued our way on to the Village upon the Seavern. Where the Fellow told me there was an honnest Gentlemen, one Mr. Woolfe that lived in that Towne, where I might be with greate safety for that he had hideing holes for Preists. But I would not goe in, till I knew a little of his minde, whether he would receive soe dangerous a Guest as me; and therefore stayed in a Feild under a hedge by a greate Tree,

[4] Replacing "the."
[5] Replacing "greate."

had commerce with France that I might get over that way I thinking that none would suspect my being gone that way. And remembering several honest gentlemen of Wales that way that were of my acquaintance.

So that night as soon as it was dark *Rd Pend.* and I took our journey afoot towards the *Severne.* And intended to pass over at a ferry half way between *Bridge No* and *Shrewsbury.* But as we were going in the night we came by a *Mill* where we heard some people talking (⟨*Memd* that⟩ I got some bread and cheese that night before at *Rd P's* ⟨one of the *P's* houses⟩ house I not going in) and as we conceived it was pretty late (12 or 1 at night) the country fellow desired me not to answer if any body asked me any Question because I had not the accent of the country. Just as we came to the mill we could see the miller (as I believed) sitting at the mill door he being in whitish clothes it being a very dark night. And he called out who goes [7] there. Upon which R P answered neighbours going home or such like words. Upon which the miller cried if you be neighbours, stand ⟨or else I will knock you down⟩. But we believing that there was company in the house the fellow bid me fallow him close and he run to a gate that went up a durty lane up a hill and opened the gate upon which the miller cried out rogues rogues and there came out some men out of the mill ~~for~~ after us which I believed were soldiers. But we fell a running up the durty lane both of us as long as we could run. It being very deep and very durty till at last I bid him leap over a hedge and lie still to hear if any body fallowed us. Which we did and laid down upon the ground about half an hour to hear if any body fallowed us. ~~Which we did and laid down upon the ground~~ And hearing no body come we continued our way on to the village upon the *Severne.* So the fellow told me that there was a very honest gentleman one Mr. *Wolfe* that lived in the town where I might ~~lay~~ be very safely. For he had hiding holes there for priests. But I would [8] not go in till I knew a little of his mind. Whether he would ~~undertake~~ receive so dangerous a guest as me. And stayed in a field ~~near~~ under a hedge by a great tree commanding him not to say it was I, but only to ask Mr. Woolf whether he would receive an English Gentleman, a person of Quallity, to hide him on the next day till we could travel againe by night, for I durst not goe but by Night.

Mr. Woolf, when the Country-Fellow told him that it was one that had escaped from the Battle of Worcester, said, that for his part it was soe dangerous a thing to harbour any boddy that was knowne, that he would not venture his Neck for any man, unless it were the King himselfe. Upon which Richard Penderell very indiscreetly, and without any Leave, told him that it was I. Upon which, Mr. Woolfe replyed, that he should be very redy to venture all he had in the World to Secure me.

Upon which, Richd. Penderell came and told me what he had done, at which I was a little troubled; but then there was noe remedy, they [*sic*] day being just comeing on, and I must either venture that or runn some greater danger.

Soe I came into the House a Back way, where I found Mr. Woolfe, an Old Gentleman, who told me he was very sorry to see me there, because there was 2 Companyes of the Militia-Foote at that time in Armes in the Towne, and kept a Guard at the Ferry to examine every boddy that came that way, in expectacion of catching some that might be makeing their escape that way. And that he durst not put me into any of the hideing-holes of his House, because they had beene discovered, and consequently, if any search should be made, they would certainly repaire to those [6] holes. And that therefore I had noe other way of Security but to goe into his Barne * and there lye behinde his Corne and Hay. Soe after he had given us some cold meate that was ready, we (without makeing any Bustell in the House) went away and lay in the Barne all the next day, when towards Evening, his sonn who had beene Prisoner at Shrewsbury, an Honnest man, was released and came home to his Fathers-House; and as soone as ever it begun to be a little darkish, Mr. Woolf and his Sonn, brought us meate into the Barne, and there we discoursed with them whether we might safely gett over the Severne into Whales. Which they advised me by noe means to adventure upon, because of the Strict Guards that were kept all along the Severne where

[6] Replacing "the."

~~and when R P in~~ commanding him not to tell that it was I but to ask him whether he would receive an English man a person of quality to hide ⟨him⟩ all next day till we could travel again by night for I durst not go but by night.

Mr. *Wolfe* when the country fellow told him that ~~this~~ ⟨that it was one⟩ that had escaped from the battle of *Worsestr* he said that for his part ~~that~~ it was so dangerous a thing to harbour any body that was known that he would not venture his neck for any body unless it was the king himself. Upon which R P very indiscreetly and without my ~~live~~ leave told him it was I. ~~He came the~~ ⟨Upon which⟩ Mr. W ~~told tell~~ told him that he should be very ready to venture all he had in the world to secure me.

Upon which R P came and told me what he had done. At which I was a little troubled but then there was no remedy ~~that~~ the day being just coming on and I must venture that or run a [9] a greater danger.

So I came into the house a back way where I find Mr. W an old gentleman who told me that he was very sorry to see me there because that there was 2 ~~or 3~~ companies of foot at that time of the militia that were in arms there in the town and they had a ~~guard~~ guard at the ferry ~~there~~ boat to examine every body that ~~sh~~ came that way. Believing that some might escape that way. And he durst not ~~to~~ put me into any of the hiding holes of his house because they had been discovered ~~because~~ ⟨and so⟩ if any came to search there they would ~~see~~ certainly go ~~into~~ to them. And that therefore ~~he~~ I had no other way but to go down in his barn and lie ~~under~~ behind the corn and hay. ~~In which~~ So after he had given ~~me~~ us some ~~⊥~~ cold meat ~~he could make~~ that was ready without ⟨making⟩ any bustle in the house we went and lay there in the barn all the next day and towards evening his son who was then prisoner at Shrewsbury being an honest man was released and came home to his father's house. [10] And as soon as ever it begun to be a little darkish Mr. W and his son brought us meat into the barn and there we talked with him whether it were easy to get over Severn into Wales which they advised me by no means to do because that there was strict guards all along upon any Passage could be found for preventing any Boddyes escapeing that way into Whales.

Upon this, I tooke Resolucion of goeing that night the very [7] same way back againe to Penderells-House, where I knew I should hear Some Newes what was become of my Lord Willmott, and resolved againe upon goeing for London.

Soe, we sett out as soon as it was dark.* But as we came by the Mill again, we had noe mind to be questioned a second time there; and therefore asking Richard Penderell whether he could Swimm or noe, and how deep the River was, he told me it was a Scurvey River, not easy to be past in all places, and that he could not swimm. Soe I told him that the River being but a little one I would undertake to help him over. Upon which we went over some Closes to the River-side, and I entering the River first to see whither I could my selfe goe over, who knew how to swim, found it was but a little above my middle; and thereupon takeing Richard Penderell by the hand, I helped him over.

Which being done, we went ⟨on⟩ our way to one of Penderells Brothers * (his house being not farr from White-Ladyes) who had been guide to my Lord Willmott, and we beleived might by that time be come back againe. For my Lord Willmott intended to goe to [8] London upon his owne Horse. When I came to this House, I enquired where My Lord Willmott was; it being now towards Morning, and haveing travelled these two Nights on Foote. Penderells Brother told me, that he had conducted him to a very honest Gentlemans House, one Mr. Pitchcroft,* not farr from Woolverhampton, a Romane Catholick. I asked him, What News? He told mee that there was one Major Careless in the House that was that Country-Man; whome I knowing, he haveing beene a Major in our Army and made his Escape thither, a Roman Catholick also, I sent for him into the Roome where I was; and consulting with him what we should doe the next day, he told me; that it would be very dangerous for me either to stay in that House or to goe into the Wood (there being a greate Wood hard by Boscobell), that he knew but one way how to pass the next day, and that was to get up into a greate Oake in a pretty plaine place, where we might see round about us; for the

[7] Replacing "way."
[8] Replacing "for."

the Severn where any body could get over for fear of any body escaping that way into Wales.

Upon this I took ~~the~~ a resolution to go that night back again the same way we came and to go to Penderell's house where I knew I should hear some news what was become of my Lord *Willmott* and resolved again of going away for London. So we set out as soon as it was dark ~~intend~~ but as we came by this mill again we had no mind to be ~~examined~~ questioned there a 2^d time and so I asked *Rd P* whether he could ~~swim~~ swim or no and how deep the river was. He said it was a scurvy river and not easy to be passed in all places and he could not swim so I told him that [11] the river being but a little one I would undertake to help him over. So we went over some closes to the river side and I went in first into the river to see whether I could go ~~out~~ over myself. Knowing how to swim. And I found it was ~~not~~ but a little above my middle and so I took him by the hand and helped him over.

So away we went on our way. And went to one of *Pendlls* brothers (*Pendlls* house was not far off from White Ladies) who had been guide to my Lord *Willmott* and we believed might be come back again. For my Lord *W* intended to go to London upon his own horse. When he ~~came~~ I came to this house I enquired where my Lord *W* was. Which was towards morning (having travelled those two nights afoot) and *Pendlls* brother told me that he had conducted him to a very honest gentleman's house one Mr. ~~Pitcheroft~~ *Whitgrave*[4] not far from *Wolv*.hampton a catholic. I asked him what news he told me that there was one *Majr. Carles* in the house then [12] in the house a sl that was that country man and I knowing him he having been a major in our army and had made his escape thither and a catholic I ~~went~~ sent for him into the room where I was. So we were consulting together what we should do the next day. He told me that it would be very dangerous either to stay in the house or go into the wood (there being a great wood hard by *Boskobell*) and he knew but one way ~~house~~ how to pass all the next day and that was to get up ~~and~~ into a great *Oake* in a pretty plain place where we could see round about us for they would certainly search all

[4] Pepys probably made this correction (which is not in his transcription) after interviewing Father Huddleston.

Enemy would certainly Search all the Wood for People that had made their Escape. Of which Proposicion of his I approveing, we (that is to say Careless and I) went and carryed up with us some Victualls for the whole day, vizt, Bread, Cheese, Small Beere, and nothing Elce, and got up into a greate Oake that had been Lop't some 3 or 4 Yeares before, and being growne out again very Bushy and Thick, could nott be seene through. And heere we stay'd all the day, I haveing in the meane tyme sent Penderells Brother * to Mr. Pitchcrofts to know whether my Lord Willmott was there or noe, and had Word brought me by him at Night that my Lord was there, that there was a very Secure hideing hole in Mr. Pitchcrofts House, and that he desired me to come thether to him.*

Memorandum: That while we were in this Tree we see soldiers goeing up and downe in the thickest of the Wood, searching for persons escaped, we seeing them now and then peeping out of the Woods.

That night, Richd. Penderell and I went to Mr. Pitch-crofts,* about 6 or 7 myles off, where I found the Gentleman of the House, and an old Grandmother * of his, and Father Hurlstone, who had then the care as Governor of bringing up two Young Gentlemen, who I thinck, were Sir Jo. Preston and his Brother, they being Boyes.*

Here I spoke with my Lord Willmott, and sent him away to Coll. Lanes about 5 or 6 Myles off to see what meanes could be found for my escapeing towards London; who told my Lord, after some consultacion thereon, that he had a sister * that had a very fair pretence of goeing hard by Bristoll to a Cousen of hers that was marryed to one Mr. Norton who lived 2 or 3 Myles beyond [9] Bristoll, on Sommersettshire-side, and she might carry me thether as her Man; And from Bristoll I might finde Shipping to gett out of England.

Soe the next night I went away to Coll. Lanes,* where I changed my Cloathes into a little better habitt like a Serveing-man, being a kinde of grey Cloath suit; and the next day Mrs. Lane and I tooke our journey towards Bristoll, resolveing to lye at a place called Longmarson in the Vale of Esham.

But we had not gone two howres on our Way, But the

[9] Replacing "towards."

the wood for people that had made their escape. Of which I approved and we ⟨that is *Carlos* and I⟩ went and carried some victuals up with ~~me~~ us (only bread and cheese and small beer) for the whole day ~~I~~ and got up into a great *Oake* that had been lopped some 3 or 4 years before and so was grown out very bushy and thick not to be seen through. And ~~so~~ there we sot all the day. ~~At night~~ In this meantime I had sent ~~this~~ P's brother [13] to Mr. *Pitchcroffts* to know whether my Lord *W* was there or no. And he brought me word at night that he was there and that there was a very secure hiding hole in the house and desired me to come thither.

~~So~~ While we were in the tree we see soldiers going up and down in the thickest of the wood searching for men that were escaped. We see ~~them~~ there now and then peeping out of the woods.

So we ~~went~~ *Rd P* and I went that night to Mr. *Pitchcrofts* about 6 or 7 mile off where I found ~~my~~ the gentleman of the house and ~~his~~ an old ~~grand~~ mother of his and Father *Hurdlestone* who had then the care of bringing up ~~a~~ 2 young gentlemen I think *Sr. John Preston* and his brother ~~2~~ boys and Father *H* was their governor.

~~So there I stayed~~

Here I spoke with my Lord *W* and sent him away to *Coll. Lanes* about ~~him~~ 5 or 6 mile off to see what means I could get for to ~~have~~ make my escape towards London. My Lord *W* [14] consulting with him said that he had a sister that had a very fair pretence of going hard by *Bristoll* to a cousin of hers that was married to one Mr. Norton. Who lived 2 ~~mile~~ or 3 miles beyond *Br.* on the Somerset shire side. And she might carry me thither as her man and from *Br.* I might find shipping to get out of England.

So the next night I went away to *Coll. Lanes* where I changed my clothes [5] into a little better habit like a serving man a kind of gray cloth suit and the next day ~~we~~ Mrs. *Lane* and I took our journey towards [6] ⟨*Br*⟩ resolving to lie at a place called *Long Marson* in the vale of *Esham* and as we were ~~going~~ coming near

---

[5] Shorthand literally "close."
[6] Shorthand literally "tord."

Mare I rode on cast a Shooe, soe we were forced to ride to gett another Shooe at a Scattering Villiage, whose name begins with something like Long ———; * and as I was holding my Horses Foot, I asked the smyth What Newes? He told me that there was noe newes that he knew of since the good newes of the beateing of the Rogues, the Scotts. I asked him whether there was none of the English taken that joyned with the Scotts. He answered that he did not heere that that Rogue Charles Steward was taken, but some of the others he said were taken, but not Charles Steward. I told him that if that Rogue were taken he deserved to be hanged more then all the rest for bringing in the Scotts. Upon which he said that I spoake like an honnest man, and soe we parted.

Here it is to be noted, that we had in company with us Mrs. Lanes Sister, who was marryed to one Mr. ———,* she being then goeing to my Lord Pagetts hard by Windsor; Soe as we were to part, as accordingly we did, at Stradford upon Avon.

But a myle before we came to Stradford upon Avon,* we espied upon the way a Troop of Horse whose riders were alighted, and the Horses eateing some grass by the wayside, staying there (as I thought) while their Muster-Maister was provideing their Quarters; Mrs. Lanes Sisters Husband (who went along with her as farr as Stradford) seeing this Troop of Horse just in our way, sayd, that for his part he would not goe by them, for he had been once or twice beaten by some of the Parliament Soldiers, and he would not Runn the venture again. I heareing him say soe begg'd Mrs. Lane softly in her Eare, that we might not turne back but goe on, for that the Enemy would certainly send after us to enquire who we were, if they should see us turne. But all she could say in the world would not doe, but her Brother-in-law turned quite round and went into Stradford another way, the troop of Horse being there just getting on Horse-back about twice 12 score off, and I told her we did meete the Troop just but in the Towne of Stradford.

But then her Brother and we parted, he goeing his way and we ours towards Long-marson, where we lay at a kindsman's, I thinck of Mrs. Lane's, neither the said Kindsman nor her aforesaid brother in Law knowing who I was.*

Stratford upon *Avon* * ⁷ where we were to go over the *Avon* we
had in our company with us Mrs. *Lanes* sister who was married to
one Mr. ——— (she was going to my Lord *Pagetts* hard by
Windsor and we were to part and did part at *Stratfd* upon *Avon*)
but a mile before we came to *Stratfd* upon *A* we ~~espied~~ espied
upon the high way a troop of horse that was [15] lighted off their
horses ~~who~~ letting their horses eat some grass that was just upon
the way side. Staying there as I thought while their ~~master~~ master
was making their quarters.

~~This gent~~

Mrs. *Lanes* sister's husband that went ~~with~~ along with her
as far as *Stratfd.* seeing this troop of horse just in our way said
that for his part he would not go by them for he had been once or
twice beaten by some of the Parliaments soldiers and he would
not run that venture again. I hearing him say so I ~~said~~ begged
Mrs. *L* saftly in her ear that we might not ~~go~~ turn back but go on
for the enemies would send to enquire who we were if they see
us turn. But all she could say in the world would not do. But her
brother in law turned quite round and ~~go~~ went into Stratford
another away and the troop of horse was just getting a horse back
about twice 12 score off. And as I told her ~~we~~ we did meet the
troop just ~~but just~~ but in the town of *Stratfd.* But then we
continued on ~~his~~ our way and her brother went on his way and
we to Long Marston [16] where we lay at a kinsman's I think of
Mrs. *L's* where ~~the next day~~ I was not known but passed for Mrs.
Lanes servant. Nor ~~ded~~ did her brother ⟨in⟩ law know who I was.

~~The next day we went away to Cicester.~~

* But we had not gone 2 hours on our way but the mare
that I rid on cast a shoe so we were forced to ride to get another
shoe to a smith ~~to~~ at a scattering village ~~being~~ beginning with a
name like *Long* ———and as I was holding my horse's foot I
asked the smith what news he told me that there was no news that
he knew of since the good news of the beating of the rogues the
Scotts. I asked him if there was none of the English taken that
jined with the Scots and he answered he did not hear that that
rogue Charles *Stuart* was taken. Some of the others he said were
taken but not *Ch. St.* I ~~act~~ told ⟨him⟩ that if that rogue was taken

---

⁷ This asterisk, which appears in the manuscript, refers to a
similarly marked passage on page 16 which has been transferred to this
position in Pepys's transcription.

The next night we lay at Cicester,* and soe from thence to Mr. Nortons * House beyond Bristoll; where as soone as I ever came, Mrs. Lane called the Buttler of the House, a very honest fellow, whose name was Pope, and had served Tom Germain, a Groome of my Bedd-chamber when I was a Boy at Richmond; * she bad him to take care of Wm. Jackson (for that was my name), as haveing been lately sick of an Ague, whereof she said I was still [10] weake and not quite [11] recovered; and the trueth is, my late Fatigues and want of meate had indeed made me looke a little pale. Besides, this Pope had been a Trooper in the King my Fathers Army, but I was not to be knowne in that house for any thing but Mrs. Lanes Servant.

Memorandum: that one Mr. Lassells * a Cousen of Mrs. Lanes, went all the way with us from Coll. Lanes on Horse-back single, I rideing before Mrs. Lane.

Pope the Butler tooke greate care of me that night, I not eateing as I should have done with the Servants, upon Account of my not being well.*

The next morning I arrose pretty early, haveing [12] a very good Stomach, and went to the Buttery-Hatch to gett my Breakefast, where I found Pope and 2 or 3 other men in the roome, and we all fell to eateing bread and Butter, to which he gave us very good Ale and Sack. And as I was sitting there, there was one that looked like a Country fellow satt just by me, who talking gave soe particular [13] an Account of the Battle of Worcester to the rest of the Company, that I concluded he must be one of Cromwells Soldiers. But I asking him how he came to give soe good an Account of that Battle, he told me that he was in the Kings Regiment. By which I thought he meant one Coll. Kings Regiment. But [14] questioning him further, I perceived that he had beene in my Regiment of Guards in Major Broughtons Company, that was my Major in the Battell. I asked him what a kinde of man I was, to which he answered by describeing exactly both my Cloathes and my Horse and then lookeing upon me he told me that the King was at least 3 fingers taller than I. Upon which I

[10] Replacing "not yet."
[11] Replacing "yet."
[12] Replacing "in the morning."
[13] Replacing "good."
[14] Replacing "by."

he deserved to be hanged more then all the rest ~~of~~ for bringing in the Scots. So he told me that I spoke like an honest man and so we parted.

So we went and lay at *Cicester* the next night and so from [17] ~~and so~~ from thence to Mr. *Norton's* house beyond *Bristoll*.

So as soon as ever I came into Mr. *N's* house Mrs. *L* called the butler of the house that was a very honest fellow whose name was *Pope* that had served *Tom Germaine* a groom of my bed chamber ~~that~~ and had served him when I was a boy at *Richmond* and she bid him take care of *Willm.* (*Jackson*) (for that was my name) for I had been lately sick of an ague and was (yet) a little ~~yet~~ weak and not quite recovered and the great fatigue and want of meat had endeed made ~~him~~ me look a little pale. And this *Pope* had been a trooper in the king my father's army. ~~And~~ but I was not to be known in that house for any thing but Mrs. *L's* servant.

Memd that one Mr. *Lassells* a cousin of Mrs. *L's* went all the way with us a horse back by himself from *Coll L's*. I riding before Mrs. *L*.

~~The next morning~~ Pope took great care of me that night I not eating that night (as I should have done) with the servants [18] upon account of my not being well.

The next morning I rose pretty early having a very good stomach and went to the buttery hatch to get my breakfast where I found the butler *Pope* and 2 or 3 ~~others~~ other men in the room and we all fell a eating bread and butter and he gave us very good *ale* and sack. So as I was sitting there ~~in~~ there was a man that looked like a country fellow sat just by me and he talking gave an account so particular of the battle of *W* to the rest that were there that I concluded that he must be one of *Cromwells* soldiers. But I asking him how he came to give so good an account of the battle he told me that he was in the King's regiment. Which at first I thought he had meant one *Coll. King's* regiment. But I asking him further perceived that he ~~he~~ was in my regiment of guards in *Majr. Broughton's* company that was my major in the battle. ~~Which made me resolve~~ And I asked him what a kind of man I was and he ~~told me~~ described exactly my clothes and my horse and [19] then looking upon me told me that the King was at least 3 fingers taller then me. Upon which I made what haste I could made what hast I could out of the Buttery, for feare he should indeed know me, as being more afraid when I knew he was one of our owne Soldiers then when I took him for one of the Enemys.

Soe Pope and I went into the Hall, and just as we came into it Mrs. Norton was comeing by through it. Upon which, I plucking of my Hatt, and Standing with my Hatt in my hand as she past by, I observed, just as I was putting off my Hatt, that Pope looked very earnestly in my Face. But I tooke noe notice of it, but put on my Hatt againe and went away, walking out of the House into the feild.

I had not been out half an hower, but comeing back I went up to the Chamber where I lay; And just as I came thether, Mr. Lassells came [15] to me, and in a little trouble said What shall we doe? I am affraid Pope knowes you, for he says very possitively to me that it is you, but I have denyed it. Upon which I presently without more adoe asked him whether he was a very honest man or noe; whereto he answereing me that he knew him to be soe honest a fellow that he durst trust him with his Life, as haveing beene alwayes on our Side, I thought it better to trust him then goe away leaveing that Suspicion upon him; and thereupon sent for Pope and told him that I was very glad to meete him there and would trust him with my life as an Old acquaintance. Upon which, being a discreet fellow he asked me what I [16] intended to doe, for sayes he, I am extreamely happy I know you, for otherwise you might run greate danger in this House. For though my Maister and Mistress are good people, yet there are at this tyme 1 or 2 in it that are very great Rogues, and I thinck I can be usefull to you in any thing you will command me. Upon which, I told him my designe of getting a shipp (if possible) at Bristoll, and to that end bad him goe that very day immediately to Bristoll to see if there were any Shipps goeing either to Spain or France that I might gett a passage away in.*

I told him also that my Lord Willmott was comeing to meet me heere (for he and I had agreed at Coll. Lanes, and were to meete this ⟨very⟩ day at Nortons); * upon which, Pope told me that it was most fortunate that he knew me and had heard this

<hr/>

[15] Replacing "come."
[16] Replacing "he."

out of the buttery for fear he should know me. As being more afeared when I knew he was ~~our own our~~ one of our own soldiers then if he had been of the enemies.

So ⟨Pope and⟩ I went out into the hall and just as we came into the hall Mrs. *Norton* was coming by through the hall and I plucked off my hat and stood with my hat in my hand as she passed by. And I observed just as I put off my hat that *Pope* the butler looked very earnestly in my face. But I took no notice of it but put on my hat again and went away and walked out of the house into the field.

I had not been out half an hour but I came back up into the chamber where I lay and just as I came up into the chamber Mr. *Lassells* came up to me and ~~told~~ said to me in a little trouble *Pope* I am afeared knows you. What shall we do for ⟨he⟩ says ~~tis~~ very positively to me that it is you. But I have denied it. [20] So I presently without more ado asked him whether he was a very honest man. He told me ~~for~~ that for his part he knew him so honest a fellow (he having been always of our side) that he durst trust him with his life. Upon which I thought it better to trust him then go away with that suspicion upon him. Upon which I sent for *Pope* and told him that I was very glad to meet him there and that I would trust him with my life as an old acquaintance. Upon which being ~~dis~~ a discreet fellow he asked me what I intended to do. For says ~~he it is~~ he I am extremely happy I do know you for otherwise you might run great danger in this house. For though my master and mistress are ~~bless~~ good people. Yet there are now in this house one or two that are very great rogues and I think I can be useful in anything you will command me. Upon which I told him my design of getting a ship if possible at ~~in~~ *Br*. And to that end I bid him go immediately that day to *Br* to see if there [21] if there were any ships going either to Spain or France that I might get a passage away.

I told him that my Lord ~~R~~ *W* was coming to meet me ~~there~~ here (this I and my Lord *W* had agreed on at *Coll Lanes* and I was to meet him this very day at *Norton's*). Upon which *Pope* told me that it was most fortunate that he knew me and had heard this of me. For if my Lord *W* should have come hither he

from me, for that if my Lord Willmott should have come hither
he would have beene most certainly knowne to Severall people in
the House; and therefore he would goe and accordingly went out
and mett my Lord Willmott a Myle or two off of the House,
carrying him to an Ale-House not farr off, where he lodged him
till it was night, and then brought him hither by a back Door into
my Chamber, I still passing for a Serveing man, and Lassell's and
I lay in one Chamber, he knowing all the Way [17] who I was.

Soe after Pope had been at Bristoll to inquire for a Shipp,
but could heere of none ready to depart beyond Sea sooner then
within a Moneth, whiche was too long for me to stay thereabout,
I betooke my self to the adviseing afresh with my Lord Willmott
and Pope what was to be done and the Latter telling me that
there lived some where in that Country upon the edge of
Sommersett-shire at Trent within two Myles of Sheerburne
Franck Windham the Knight-Marshalls Brother, who being my
old acquaintance and a very honest man, I resolved to goe to his
House.

But the night before we were to goe away, we had a
misfortune that might have done us much prejudice; for Mrs.
Norton who was bigg with Child fell into Labour and miscarry'd
of a dead Child, and was very ill: Soe that we could not tell how
in the world to finde an excuse for Mrs. Lane to leave her Cousen
in that condicion; and indeed it was not safe to stay longer there,
where there was soe greate resort of disaffected Idle people.

At length consulting with Mr. Lassells I though the best
way to counterfeit a Letter from her fathers House old Mr. Lane's,
to tell her that her Father was extreamly ill and commanded her
to come away immeadiately for feare that she should not
otherwise finde him alive. Which Letter Pope delivered soe well
while they were all at Supper, and Mrs. Lane playing her part soe
dextirously, that all beleived Old Mr. Lane to be indeed in great
danger, and gave his Daughter the Excuse to goe away with me
the very next morning early.

Accordingly the next morning we went directly to Trent
to Franck Windhams house, and lay that night at Castle-Cary,*
and the next night came to Trent, where I had appointed my
Lord Willmott to meete me, whome I still tooke care not to keepe
with me, but sent him a little before or left to come after me.*

[17] Replacing "while."

would have been certainly known to several people in the house. So he went and met him a mile or 2 off of the house and carried him to an ale house not far off and there lodged him till it was night and then brought him into the house by a back way into my chamber. I still passing for a serving man. And *Lassells* and I lay in one chamber. Who knew who I was all the way.

So ~~he~~ after *Pope* had been at *Br* to enquire for a ship there was none [22] there was none that he could hear of to part beyond ~~the~~ sea sooner then within a month. Which was too long for me to stay there abouts.

Therefore I took my resolution ⟨of going to *ffr. Wyndham's*⟩ ⟨upon advising with my Lord *W* and this *Pope*, who told me ~~who~~ there lived somewhere in the country ~~somewhere~~ upon the *edge* of *Somerset* shire *ffrancke Windeham* at *Trent* within 2 mile of *Sherburne*. And he being my old acquaintance ⟨the *Kt.* Marshall's brother⟩ and a very honest man I resolved to go to his house.

~~And~~ But that night before we were to go away we had a great misfortune that might have done us great prejudice. For Mrs. *Norton* who was big with child fell into labour and was brought to bed ⟨miscarried⟩ of a dead child and was very ill so that we could not tell how in the world to have an excuse for Mrs. *Lane* to leave her cousin in that condition and it was not safe to stay longer there where there was great resort of [23] disaffected idle people.

So I ⟨consulting ~~he~~ with Mr. *Lassells*⟩ thought the best way was to counterfeit a letter from her father's house ⟨old Mr. *Lane*⟩ to send her word that he was extreme ill and commanded her to come away immediately for fear she should not find him alive. Which letter *Pope* delivered so well ~~at supper~~ while they were ⟨all⟩ at supper and Mrs *L* played her part so well that all believed that old Mr. *Lane* was in great danger of dying. And gave her an excuse to go away with me the next morning very early. So we went next morning away directly for *Trent Fr. Wyndhs.* house and lay that night at *Castle cary* ~~where they drink waters~~ and the next night we came to *Trent*.

Where I had appointed my Lord *W* to meet me. For I still kept him not with me. But a little before or to come after me.

When we came to Trent, my Lord Willmott and I advised with Franck Windham whether he had any acquaintance at any Sea-Towne upon the Coast of Dorsett or Devonshire, who told me that he was very well acquainted with Gyles Strangwayes and that he would goe directly to him and informe himselfe whether he might not have some acquaintance at Waymouth or Lime, or some of those Ports.

But Gyles Strangwayes proved not to have any, as haveing beene long absent from all those places, as not dareing to stirr abroad, haveing been always faithfull to the King; but he desired Franck Windham to try what he could doe therein himself, it being unsafe for him to be found busy upon the Sea-Coast. But with all, he sent me 300 Broad Pieces,* which he knew were necessary for me in the Condicion I was now in; for I durst carry noe money about me in those meane Cloathes and my haire cutt Short but about 10 or 12 shillings Silver.

Franck Windham upon this went himself to Lyme, and spoake with a Merchant there to hire a shipp for my Transportacion, being forced to acquaint him that it was I that was to be carryed out.* The Merchant undertooke it (his name being William Elesdon],* and accordingly hired a Vessell for France appointing a day for my comeing to Lyme to imbarke. And accordingly we sett out from Franck Windhams, and (to cover the matter the better) I road before a Cousen of Franck Windhams, one Mrs. Judith Conesby,* still goeing by the name of Wm. Jackson.

Memorandum that one day dureing my stay at Trent I heareing the Bells ring (the Church being hard by Franck Windhams house) and seeing a Company gott together in the Church yard, I sent downe the maid of the House (who knew me) to enquire what the matter was. Who returning, came up and told me; that there was a Rogue a Trooper come out of Cromwells Army that was telling the people that he had killed me, and that that was my Buffe-Coate which he had then on. Upon which most of the Villiage being Fanatiks, they were ringing the Bells and makeing a Bone-Fyer for joy of it.

This Merchant haveing appointed us to come to Lyme we (vizt. My selfe, My Lord Willmott, Franck Windham, Mrs.

So when we were come to *Trent* my Lord *W* and I advised with *Fr. W* whether he had any acquaintance with any sea town upon [24] ~~sea town~~ the coast of *Dosett* shire or *Devon* shire.

He told me that he ~~was~~ very well acquainted with *Giles Strangwayes* and that he was would go directly to *G Strangwayes* and advise with him whether he had no acquaintance in *Weymo* or *Lime* or some of those ports.

But *G St.* could not having been long from any of those places. Not daring to stir as having been always faithful to the King. He desired *Fr W* to ⟨do⟩ what he could himself as not daring to be too busy ~~upon~~ upon the sea coast but with all sent me 300 broad pieces which he knew was necessary for ~~in~~ me in that condition. For I durst carry no money about me in those mean clothes but about 10 or 12 shillings in silver. [My own hair short.] [8]

Fr. W upon this went to *Lime* himself and spoke with a merchant there to hire a ship for my transportation. And was forced to acquaint the merchant that it was I that was to be carried out of England. And the merchant undertook it and did [25] and did hire a vessel to carry me to France. (The merchant name is ⟨Limbry⟩) [9] and appointed a day for me to come to *Lime* to imbark. And we set out from *F W* accordingly and ~~I rid~~ (to cover the matter the better) I rid before a cousin of *F W* one Mrs. *Judith Connesby* still going under the name of *W Jackson*.

Memd as I was at *Trent* one day I heard the bells ring (the church being hard by *F W* house) and I see a company got together to the church yard and I sent down the ~~maid~~ mayd of the house (who knew me) to enquire what the matter was. And she came up and told me that there was a rogue a trooper that had come out of *Cromwell's* army that said that he had killed me and that that was my buff coat that he had then on. And most of that village being fanatics were ~~ringing~~ ringing the bells and making a bon fire for it.

So this *Mercht.* that appointed us to come to *Lime* [26]

---

[8] The square brackets are in the manuscript.

[9] A dash was written originally and the name was inserted later, after the transcription was made. This name is in fact the sailor's: the merchant was William Ellesdon.

Conesby, and one servant of Franck Windhams whose name was Peter *) were directed from him to a Little Village hard by Lyme,* the Vessel being to come out of the Cobb at Lyme, and come to a Little Crick that was just by this Villiage (whether we went) and to send their Boate a Shoare to take us in at the said Creck and carry us over to France, the winde being then very good at North.

Soe we satt up that Night expecting the Shipp to come out; but she fayled us. Upon which I sent Franck Windhams man Peter and my Lord Willmott to Lyme the next morning to know the reason of it.* But we were much troubled how to pass away our time the next day, till we could have an answere. At last we resolved to goe to a place on the Roade towards London called Burport,* about 4 myles from Lyme, and there stay till my Lord Willmott should bring us news whether the Vessell could be had the next night or noe, and the reason of her Last nights faylure.

Soe Franck Windham and Mrs. Conesby and I went in the morning on Horse-back away to Burport, and just as we came into the Towne, I could see the Streets full of Redd-Coates, Cromwells Soldiers (being a Regiment of Coll. Haynes's (vizt.) 1500 men going to imbarke * to take Jerzey) at which Franck Windham was very much startled, and asked me what I would doe. I told him that we [18] must goe impudently into the best inn * in the Towne and take a Chamber there, as the only thing to be done; because we should otherwise miss my Lord Willmott in case we went any whether elce, and that would be very inconvenient both to him and me. Soe we Rodd directly into the best Inn of the place and found the Yard very full of Soldiers. I alighted, and takeing the Horses thought it the best way to goe blundering in among them, and lead them through the middle of the Soldiers into the Stable, Which I did and they were very angry with me for my rudeness.

As soon as I came into the Stable I tooke the Bridles off the Horses, and called the Ostler to me to help me give the Horses some Oates.* And as the Ostler was helping me to feed the Horses, Sure, Sir (Sayes the Ostler) I know your face. Which was noe very pleasant Questian to me, but I thought the best way was to

[18] Replacing "the best way."

appointed us to come to a little village ⟨*Charmouth* [10]⟩ hard by *Lime viz.* my Lord *W* and *ff W* and Mrs. *Conisby* and I and one servant of *ffr. W's* whose name was *Peter.*

So when we came thither the ~~ship~~ vessel was to come out at the *Cobb* at *Lime* and come ~~to~~ hard by a little creek that was just by this village where we were and ~~sent~~ said their boat ashore and take us ~~up there and~~ in at the creek and carry us to France, the wind then being very good at *No.*

So we sat up that night expecting the ship to come out, but she failed us that night. Upon which, next morning I sent *ffr. W⟨'s Man Peter & my Lord Willmott⟩* to *Lime* to know the reason of it. But we were very much troubled how to pass away our time the next day till we had an answer. And we resolved at last to go to a place on the road towards *London* called *Burport,* about 4 mile from *Lime* and there stay till my Lord *W* should bring us news whether the ship could be had the next night or no and the reason of her last failure. [27]

So *ffr. W* and Mrs. *C* and I went in the morning ⟨a horseback⟩ away to *Burport* and just as we came into the town I could see all the streets full of red coats *Cromwell's* soldiers. At which *ffr. W* was very much startled and asked me what I would do. So I ~~told~~ told him that we must go impudently into the best ~~inn~~ *Inne* in the town ~~as~~ and take a chamber there as the only thing to be done. For else we should miss my Lord *W* if we went away thence, which would be very inconvenient both to him and me. So off we rid into the best inn in the town ⟨the *George* [11]⟩ ~~there~~ and there we found the yard very full of soldiers and I ⟨light and⟩ took the horses and I thought it was the best way to go blundering in ~~away~~ among them and lead them through the middle of the soldiers into the stable ~~and~~ ⟨which I did and⟩ they were angry with me for my rudeness.

So as soon as I came into the stable and took off the bridles off the horses and called the ostler to help me to give the horses some *Oates.* And as the ostler ~~looked~~ was helping me to ~~I~~ feed the [28] the horses. ~~Sir~~ Sure *Sr.* ⟨says the ostler⟩ I know your face. Which was not a very pleasant question to me but I thought the

---

[10] *"Charmouth"* was added above the line after the transcription was made.

[11] The name of the inn was added after the transcription was made.

ask him where he had lived? whether he had alwayes lived there
or noe? He told me, that he was but newly come thether, that he
was borne in Exeter and had been Ostler in an Inn there, hard by
one Mr. Potter's a Merchant, in whose House I had laine [19] in the
time of War. Soe I thought it best to give the fellow noe further
occacion of thinking where he had seen me, for feare he should
guess right at Last. Therefore I told him, Freind, Certainly you
have seene me there at Mr. Potters, for I served him a good while,
above a yeare. Oh, sayes he, then I remember you a Boy there,
and with that was putt off from thinking any more on it but
desired that we might drinck a Pott of Beere together. Which I
excused by saying that I must goe waite upon my Maister, and
gett his dinner ready for him, but told him, that my Maister was
goeing for London and would returne about three Weekes hence,
when he would lye there, and I would not faile to drink a pott
with him.

As soon as we had dined, my Lord Willmott came into the
Towne from Lyme, but went to another Inne. Upon which we
rode out of Towne as if we had gone upon the Roade towards
London, and when we were gott 2 Myle off, my Lord Willmott
overtooke us (he haveing observed while in Towne where we
were and told us that he beleived the Shipp might be ready next
night, but that there had beene Some mistake between him and
the Maister of the Shipp.

Upon which, I not thinking it fitt to goe back againe to
the same place where we had satt up the night before, we went to
a Villiage * called [Broad Windorr],[20] about 4 Myles in the
Country above Lyme, and sent in Peter to know of the Merchant
whether the shipp would be ready, but the Maister of the Shipp
doubting that it was some dangerous Employment he was hired
upon absolutely refused the Merchant, and would not undertake
to carry us over.

[19] Replacing "beene."
[20] Added in the shorthand report, but still blank in Pepys's
transcription.

best was to ask him where he had lived whether always there or
no. He told me that he had been but lately there but he was born
in Exeter and had ~~lived~~ been ostler in an *Inne* at Exeter hard by
one Mr. *Potters* ⟨a merchant⟩ in whose house I had lain in the
time of the war. So I thought it best not to ~~let the people the~~
~~fellow think~~ ⟨give occasion to the fellow to think further⟩ where
he had seen me, for fear he should guess right at last. So I told
him Friend certainly you saw me at Mr. *Potters* for I served him
a good while. Above a year. Oh says he then I remember you a
boy there and so put the fellow out of thinking any more. So he
desired me that we might drink a pot of beer together. But I
excused myself by saying that I must go wait upon my master.
And get his dinner ready for him. But I ~~promise~~ told him that my
~~master~~ master was going to London and should return about 3
weeks hence and would lie there and then I would not fail to
drink a pot of beer together with him. [29]

So after dinner as soon as we have dined my Lord *W*
came into the town from *Lime,* but he went to another *Inne* [12]
[this regiment that was there was 1500 men ~~going to~~ of *Coll:*
Harris's regiment going to ~~take J~~ imbark to take *Jerzy*].

So we rid out of town as if we had gone ~~to London~~ upon
the road toward *London,* and when we have got about 2 mile out
of town my Lord *W* overtook us ⟨he seeing ⟨in the town⟩ where
we were⟩ and told us that he believed ~~that he believed~~ the ship
might be ready next ~~night~~ night but that there ~~was~~ ⟨had been⟩
some mistake between him and the master of the ship and that he
believed the next night he would be ready for us. But I not
thinking it fit ~~for~~ to go back again to the same place where we had
sat up long the night before we went to a village that was 4 miles
in the country ~~about~~ above *Lime* called ⟨*Broad Windorr* [13]⟩ where
we lay that night and sent in Potter to know of the merchant
whether the ship would be ready. But the master of the ship
doubting that it was some dangerous imployment he was hired
upon absolutely refused the merchant and would not undertake to

[12] The first session of Pepys's report, the evening of Sunday,
October 3, 1680, ended here. The remainder was done on the morning of
the following Tuesday.

[13] A space was left originally and the name filled in after the
transcription was made. Pepys must have got the name from some other
document.

Whereupon we were forced to goe back again to Franck Windhams to Trent, where we might be in some safety, till we had hired another Shipp.*

As soone as we came to Franck Windhams, I sent away presently to Coll. Robt. Phillipps,* who lived then at Salisbury, to see what he could doe for the getting me a shipp; which he undertook very willingly, and had gott one at Southampton. But by Misfortune she was among others Prest to Transport their soldiers to Jerzey; By which she failed us alsoe.*

Upon this, I sent further into Sussex, where Robin Phillipps knew one Coll. Gunter, to see whether he could hire a Shipp anywhere upon that Coast, and not thinkeing it convenient for me to stay much Longer at Franck Windhams (Where I had beene in all about a Fortnight and was become known to very many) I went directly away to a Widdow-Gentlewomans house one Mrs. Hyde, some 4 or 5 Myles from Salisbury.* Where I came into the House just as it was almost dark (with Robin Phillipps only) not intending at first to make myselfe knowne. But just as I alighted at the Doore, Mrs. Hide knew me, though she had never seen mee but once in her life, and that was with the King my Father, in the Army, when we marched by Salisbury some yeares before in the time of the Warr. But she being a discreet Woman took noe notice at that time of me, I passing only for a freind of Robin Phillips's, by whose advice I went thether.

At supper there was with us Frederick Hyde, (since a Judge) and his sister in law a Widdow, Robin Phillips, my Selfe, and Dr. Henshaw (since Bishopp of London) * whome I had appointed to meet me there.

While we were at supper I observed Mrs. Hyde and her Brother Frederick to looke a little earnestly at me, which ledd me to beleive they might know me. But I was not at all startled at it, it haveing beene my purpose to lett her know who I was. And accordingly after supper Mrs. Hyde came to me, and I discovered my selfe to her, who told me shee had a very safe place to hide me in, till we knew whether any shipp was ready or noe. But she sayd it was not safe for her to trust any Boddy but her selfe and carry us over. Upon which we were forced to return again to *ffr W's* house to *Trent* where we might be in ~~small~~ some safety till we had hired another ship. As soon as we came to *ffr. W's* ~~we~~ I sent away [30] ~~among~~ away presently to *Coll. Rbt Phillips* who lived then at *Salsbury* to see what he could do for the getting me a ship to carry me over. Which he ~~undertook~~ undertook very willingly and had got one at *Southampton.* But by misfortune she was pressed away to help to carry some of these soldiers over to take *Jerzy.* So that ship failed us likewise.

Upon which I sent away further into *Sussex* where *Rob. Ph.* ~~knowing~~ knew one *Coll. Gunter* to see whether he could hire a ship ~~for~~ anywhere upon the coast of *Sussex.* And not thinking it convenient to stay much longer at *ffr. W's* (so many knowing of me and having stayed there in all ~~all~~ about a fortnight) I went to ~~a~~ directly away to ⟨a⟩ gentlewoman's house that was a widow one Mrs. *Hide* some 4 or 5 mile above *Salsbury.* Where I came into the house just as it was almost dark (*Rob. Ph.* and I only) where at first I did not intend to make ~~them~~ myself known. But just as I light at the door Mrs. *Hide* seeing me knew me. Though she had never seen me but once in her life and that was with the King my father in the army when we marched by *Salsbury* some years before ~~into~~ in the time of the war. But she being a discreet woman took no notice of me then. ~~At supper~~ For I passed then for a ~~cous~~ friend of *R Ph.* By whose advice I went to this house. At supper [31] ~~as we there was one Fred.~~ there was with us *Frederick Hide* (who was since a judge) and his sister in law a widow *Rob Phillips* and I and *Dr. Henshaw* ~~was~~ who was since *Bp.* of London whom I had appointed to meet me there. ⟨And Mrs. *Conisby.*[14]⟩

While we were at supper I see that Mrs. *H* looked a little earnestly at me (as ~~did also~~ her brother Mr. *ffr. Hide* ⟨also did⟩) which made me believe that they might know me. But I was not startled at all ~~because~~ at it because I did intend to let her know who I was.

So that night after supper Mrs. *Hide* came to me and I told her who I was and ~~asked her advice how I might be priv~~ she told me that she had a very safe place to hide me in till we knew whether our ship was ready or no. But she said that it was not safe

---

[14] "And Mrs. Conisby" was added later and does not appear in Pepys's transcription.

her sister; and therefore advised me to take my Horse the next morning, and make as if I quitted the House, and returne again about night. For she would order it soe, that all her servants and everybody should be out of the House but her selfe and her sister, whose name I remember not.

Soe Robin Phillipps and I tooke our Horses and went as farr as Stoneheng; and there we stayd lookeing upon the stones for sometyme, and returned back againe to Heale (the place where Mrs. Hide lived) about the howre she appointed; where I went up into the hideing hole, that was very convenient and safe, and stayd there all alone (Robin Phillipps then going away to Sallisbury) some 4 or 5 dayes, sometimes Mrs. Hide and sometimes her sister bringing me meat.

After 4 or 5 dayes stay, Robin Phillipps came to the House, and acquainted me that a Shipp was ready provided for me at Shoram, by Coll. Gunter. Upon which, at two a Clock in the Morning I went out of the House by the back way, and with Robin Phillipps mett Coll. Gunter and My Lord Willmott together some 14 or 15 Myles off on my way towards Shoram,* and were to lodge that night at a place called Hammelton,* 7 Myles from Portsmouth, because it was too long a Journey to goe in one day to Shoram. And here we lay at a House of a Brother in Law of Coll. Gunters, one Mr. [Symonds].* Where I was not to be known (I being still in the same grey Cloath-Suite as a Serveing man), though the Maister of the House was a very honest poor man, who while we were at supper, came in, he haveing been ⟨all the day⟩ playing the Good Fellow at an Ale-House in the Towne; and takeing a stoole, satt downe with us, where his Brother in Law Coll. Gunter talking very feelingly concerning Cromwell

for her to trust any body but herself and her sister and therefore
desired me to ~~go~~ take my horse next ~~morning~~ morning and make
as if I quitted the house and return again about noon. For she
would order the matter so that all her servants and' every body
should be out of the house but herself and sister (whose name I
remember not) so *R Ph.* and I took our horses (with Mrs. *C*
behind the king) [15] and went as far as *Stonege* and there we
looked upon the stones ~~there~~ for some time and returned back
again to *Heale* [32] the place where Mrs. *Hide* lived about the
hour she appointed.

    J C here left the king in the fields and forgetting the gold
which she carried and carried him back again and with a second
kiss went away.[16]

    Where I went up ~~to~~ into the hiding hole that was very
convenient and very safe. Where I stayed some 4 or 5 days (*R Ph*
then going away to *Salsb.* so I was then alone there) sometimes
Mrs. *Hide* bringing me meat thither and sometimes her sister.

    After 4 or 5 days stay *R Ph* came to the house and
acquainted me that the ship was ready provided at *Shoram.* By
Coll. Gunter. So at 2 a clock in the morning I went out of the
house the back way and *R Ph.* and I went and met *Coll. Gunther*
some ~~miles~~ 14 or 15 miles off on my way towards *Shoram* where
we met with my Lord *W* and *Coll. Gunter* together. So that night
we were to lodge at a place called *Hamleton* 7 miles off of
Portsmo because it was too long a journey to go in one day to
Shoram. Where we lay at a house of *Coll. Gunter's* brother in law
one Mr.   where I was not to be known ~~(in~~ (still in)
the same gray suit of clothes of a serving man all the time)
though the man was a very honest poor man.

    While we were at supper the master of the house came in
who had been ~~away~~ [33] ~~who had a meal~~ been merry all the day
in an ale house in the town. So he came and took a stool and sat
down and talking his brother ~~(C Gunter~~ in law *C. Gunter*)

[15] This phrase was added later and may be inaccurate, for Phillips
states that the lady left in the morning. It does not appear in Pepys's
transcription.
  [16] This paragraph is added in shorthand at the top of the page. It is
not included in Pepys's transcription and no indication is given of its exact
place in the narrative.

and all his party, he went and whispered his brother in the Eare, and asked whether I was not some Round-headed Roagues sonn for I looked very suspitiously.* Upon which Coll. Gunter answereing for me, that he might trust his Life in my hands, he came and tooke me by the hand, and drinking a good Glass of Beere to me called me, Brother Round head.

About that time my Lord Southampton that was then at Titchfield suspecting (for what reason I don't know) * that it was possible I might be in the Country, sent either to Robin Phillipps or Dr. Henshaw to offer his service if he could serve me in my Escape. But being then provided of a Shipp, I would not put him to the danger of haveing anything to doe with it.

The next day we went to a place 4 myles off of Shoram, called Bright-Hempson, where we were to meete with the Maister of the shipp, as thinking it more convenient for us to meet there, then just at *Shoram* where the shipp was. Soe when we came to the Inn at Bright-Hempson, we mett with (one [Francis Mancell]*) the Merchant who had hired the Vessell in Company with her Maister, the Merchant only knowing me, as haveing hired her only to carry over a person of Quallity that was escaped from the Battell of Worcester, without nameing any Boddy. And as we were all * (vizt. Robin Phillipps,* my Lord Willmott, Coll. Gunter, the Merchant, the Maister and I) I observed that the maister of the vessell looked very much upon me. And as soon as we had supped, calling the Merchant aside, the Maister told him that he had not dealt fairly with him: for though he had given him a very good price for the carrying over that Gentleman, yet he had not been cleare with him, for says he, he is the King, and I very well know him to be soe. Upon which the Merchant denying it, saying that he was mistaken, the Maister answered, I know him very well, for he tooke my ship, together with other fishing Vessells at Bright-Hempson in the yeare *1648* (which was when I commanded the King my Fathers Fleete, and I very kindly lett them goe againe). But sayes he to the Merchant, be not troubled at it, for I thinck I doe God and my Country good service in preserveing the King, and by the grace of God I will venture my life and all for him, and sett him safely on shoare (if I can) in France.* Upon which the Merchant came and told me what had talking very feelingly concerning *Cromwell* and all his party he went and whispered his brother and asked if I was not some round-headed rogue's son for I looked very ~~suspicious and all~~ suspiciously. So *C. Gunter* answered for me that he might trust his life in my hands. Upon which he came and ~~drank a~~ took me by the hand and drank a good glass of beer to me and called me brother Round head.

About that time my Lord *Southampton* that was then at *Tichfield* suspecting (for what reason I dont know) that it was possible I might be in that country. Sent either to *R Ph* or *Dr. Henshaw* to offer his service if he could serve me in my escape. But I being provided them of a ship ~~and~~ would not put him to the danger of having any thing to do with it.

The next day we went to a place 4 miles off of *Shoram* called *Br. hempson*. Where we were to meet with the master of the ship that was to carry me over. Thinking it more convenient to ~~meet~~ meet there then just at *Shoram* where the ship was. So when we came to the *Inne* at *Br Hempson* we met with the merchant who had [34] hired the ship and the master. The merchant ~~only knowing me~~ (whose name is   ) only knowing me. The master being only hired to carry over a person of quality that was escaped from the battle of Worcester. ~~And~~ So as we ~~was~~ were all at supper (*R Ph. Ld W. C. Gunter* the merchant and master and I) I observed that the master of the vessel looked very much upon me and as soon as we had supped the master called the merchant aside and told him that he had not dealt fairly with him. For though he had given a very good price for to carry that gentleman over. Yet he had not ~~been in~~ been clear with him for he said it was the King, for he knew him very well. ~~For after the making~~ (Upon which) merchant denying it and saying he was mistaken. The master answered I know him very well for he took my ship with some other fishermen off *Br. Hempson* in *48* (when I commanded the King my ~~self fathers~~ father's fleet and I very kindly let them all go again) but says he to the merchant be not troubled for I think I do God and my country good service in preserving the King and by the grace of God I will venture life and all for him. And set ~~if~~ him safely ashore if I can in France.

Upon which the merchant came and told me what had

past between them; and thereby found my selfe under a necessity of trusting him. But I tooke noe kinde of notice of it presently to him; But thinking it convenient nott to lett him goe home, least he should be asking advice of his wife or any Boddy elce, we kept him with us in the Inn, and satt up all night drinking beer and takeing Tobacco with him.

And heer I also run another very greate danger, as being confident I was knowne by the Maister of the Inn.* For as I was standing after supper by the Fire-Side, leaneing my hand upon a Chaire (and all the rest of the Company being gon into another Roome) the Maister of the Inn came in and fell a-talking with me, and just as he was looking about and saw there was noe boddy in the roome, he upon a suddain kissed my hand that was upon the back of the Chaire, and said to me, God bless you, where soe ever you goe; I doe not doubt before I dye but to be a Lord, and my Wife a Lady. Soe I laughed and went away into the next Roome, not desireing then any further discourse with him, there being noe Remedy against my being known by him, and more discourse might but have raised suspicion. On which consideracion I thought it best for to trust him in that manner, and he proved very honest.

About 4 a Clock in the morning, my selfe and the Company before named went towards Shoram, takeing the Maister of the Shipp with us on horseback behinde one of our Company, and came to the Vessells side, which was not above 60 Tunn. But it being low Water, and the Vessell lying dry, I and my Lord Willmott gott up with a Ladder into her and went and lay downe in the little Cabbin, till the tide came to fetch us off.

But I was noe sooner gott into the Shipp and Layn downe upon the Bedd, but the Maister came in to me, fell downe upon his Knees and kist my hand, telling me that he knew me very well, and that he would venture Life and all that he had in the World to sett me downe safe in France.

Soe about 7 a Clock in the Morning it being High-Water we went out of the Port. But the Maister being bound for Poole laden with Sea Coole,* because he would not have it seene from Shoram, that he did not goe his intended Voyage; but stood all

passed between them [35]. So then I was forced to trust him. But
I took no kind of notice of it ~~and~~ ⟨presently but⟩ thinking it
convenient not to let him go home ~~and~~ ⟨lest he should⟩ advise
with his wife or any body else we kept him all that night with us
in the *Inne* drinking beer and tobacco with him. ~~And about 4 a~~
~~clock in the morning~~

Besides. I run a great danger. For I am confident ~~that~~ I was
known by the master of the *Inne* that proved a very honest fellow.
For as I was standing after supper by the fire side leaning my
hands upon a chair (and all ~~the company~~ the rest of the company
being gone into another room) the master of the *Inne* came in
and fell a talking with me and just as he looked ~~out~~ about and
see there was no body in the room. Of a sudden he kissed my
hand that was upon the back of the chair and said to me. God
bless you where ever you go. I do not doubt before I die but to be
a lord and my wife to be a lady. So I laughted and went away into
the next ~~morn~~ room. Not desiring ⟨then⟩ any further discourse
with him there ~~being no remedy.~~ ⟨Therefore being no remedy
against my being known by him and more discourse might have
~~discovered~~ raised suspicion⟩.

About 4 clock in the morning ⟨I and the company before
named⟩ ~~we~~ went towards *Shoram* ~~C. G.~~ ⟨being mounted⟩ ~~who~~
~~was with us. The master and we took~~ ⟨taking⟩ the master of the
ship with us behind one of our company a horse back. [36] And
came to the vessel's side that was not above 60 tons. And it being
low water the vessel lying dry I ⟨and my Lord *W*⟩ got up with a
lather into the ship and went and lay in the little cabin till the
tide came to fetch us off.

I was no sooner come into the ship and lain down upon
the bed but the master came in to me and fell down and kissed
my hand and told me that he knew me very well and that he
would venture life and all that he had in the world to set me safe
in France.

So about 7 a clock in the morning it being high water we
~~set~~ went out of the port.

But the master being bound for *Poole* laden with ⟨Sea⟩
Coles would not stand his course over to France. Because he
would ~~cast~~ not have it seen from *Shoram* that he did not go ~~to~~ his

the day with a very easy sayle toward the Isle of Weight (only my Lord Willmott and my selfe of my Company on board), and as we were sayleing the Maister came to me and desired me that I would perswade his Men to use their endeavours with me to gett him to sett us on shoare in France, the better to cover him from any suspicion thereof. Upon which I went to the Men (which were 4 and a Boy) * and told them, truely, that we were 2 Merchants that had some misfortunes and were a Little in Debt, that we had some money owing us at Roan in France and were afraid of being arrested in England, that if they would perswade the Maister (the Winde being very faire) to give us a Tripp over to Diepe or one of those ports neere Roan, they would oblige us very much; and with that I gave them 20s to drinck. Upon which they undertook to second me if I would propose it to the Maister. soe I went to the Maister and told him our condicion, and that if he would give us a Tripp over to France, we would give him Consideracion [21] for it. Upon which, he counterfeited difficulty, saying that it would hinder his Voyage. But his men, as they had promised me, Joyned their perswacions to ours, and at last he yeilded to sett us over.

Soe about 5 a Clock in the afternoone (as we were in sight of the Isle of Wight) we stood directly over for the Coast of France, the Winde being then full North; and the next morning a little before day we saw the Coast. But the tyde fayling us and the Winde comeing about to the South-West, we were forced to come to an Anchor within 2 Myles of the shoare, till the tide of Flood was done.

We found our selves just before an Harbour in France called Feckham, and just as the tyde of Ebb was made, espied a Vessell to Leeward of us, which by her nimble working I suspected to be an Ostend-Privateer. Upon which I went to my Lord Willmott, and telling him my oppinion of that shipp proposed to him [22] our goeing a Shoare in the Little Cock-Boate, for feare they should prove soe, as not knowing but finding us goeing into a Port of France (there being then a Warr between France and Spaine) they might plunder us and possibly carry us

---

[21] Replacing "some."
[22] Replacing "goe."

intended *Voyage.* But stood all the day with a very easy sail towards the *Isle* of *Wight* (only my Lord *W* and I on board) and so as we were sailing the master came to me and desired me that I would cast not have it seen from *Shoram* that he did not go to his him to set us on shore in France to cover ~~his~~ him the better from any suspicion. Upon which I went to the men (which were 4 men and a boy) and told them [37] and told them ~~to tell~~ ~~them~~ truly that we were two merchants that had some misfortune and were a little in debt. That we had some money owing us at *Roone* in France and ~~so~~ that we were afeared of being arrested in England. That if they would persuade the master (the wind being then very fair) to give us a trip over to *Diepe* or one of those ports near *Roone.* They would oblige us ~~very~~ very much, and I gave them 2o^s to drink. Upon which they undertook to ~~persuade the maister~~ second me if I would propose it to the master. So I went to ~~him~~ the master and told ~~them~~ him our condition and that if he would give us a trip to France we would give him consideration for it. ~~So the men~~ Upon which he counterfeited some difficulty. As that it would hinder his voyage. But his men (as they had promised) persuaded him and he at last yielded to set us over.

So about 5 a clock in the afternoon (as we were in sight of the *Isle* of *Wight*) we stood directly over for the coast of France. The wind being then full *No.* And the next morning a little before day we see the coast. But the tide failing us and the wind coming about [38] about to the *S W* we were forced to come to an anchor within 2 mile of the shore till the tide of ~~flood~~ flood was done.

We found ourselfs just before a harbour in France called *ffeckam.* Just as the tide of *ebb* ~~begun~~ was made we spied ~~a ship~~ ~~to leew~~ a vessel to leeward of us that I suspected to be an *Ostend* privateer by her nimble working. So I went to my Lord *W* and I told him what my opinion was of that ship and therefore desired him that we might go ashore in the little cock boat for fear it might be a *Ostendr.* and if he found us going into a port of France I did not know what he might do. He might ~~fl~~ plunder us

away and sett us a-shoare in England; the Maister also himselfe
had the same opinion of her [23] being an Ostender, and came to me
to tell me soe. Which though I made it my business to diswade
him from, for feare it should tempt him to sett sayle back againe
with us for the Coast of England, yet soe sensible I was of it that I
and my Lord Willmott went both on shoare in the Cock-Boate,
and goeing up into the Towne of Feckham stayed there all that
Day to provide Horses for Roan. But the Vessell which had soe
affrighted us proved afterwards only a French sloop.

The next day we gott to Roan to an Inn (one of the best
in the Towne) in the Fish-Markett, where they made difficulty to
receive us, takeing us by our Cloathes to be some Theeves, or
persons that had beene doeing some very ill thing, untill Mr.
Sandburne a Merchant (for whome I sent) came and answered
for us.

One perticuler more there is observable in Relacion to this
our Passage into France, that the Vessell that brought us over had
noe sooner Landed me, and I given her Maister a Pass, for feare of
meeting with any of our Jerzey-Friggates, but the Winde turned
soe happily for her as to carry her directly for Poole, without its
being knowne that she had ever beene upon the Coast of France.*

We stayd at Roan * one day to provide our selves better
Cloathes and give notice to the Queene my Mother (who was
then at Paris) of my being safely Landed. After which setting out
in a hired coach I was mett by my Mother with Coaches short of
Paris, and by her conducted thither, where I safely arived.*

Notes referring to the Severall Passages.

Page [40].

There was 6 Brothers of the Penderells, who all of them knew
the Secrett (and as I have since Learned from one of them) the man
in whose House I changed my Cloathes came to one of them about 2
days after, and asking him where I was told him that I might gett
1000 *li* if they would tell (because there was that summe layd upon
my head). But this Penderell was soe honest, that though he at that
tyme knew where I was, he bad him have a care what he did, for that
I being gott out of all reach, if they should now discover I had ever
been there, they would gett nothing but hanging for their Paynes.

[23] Replacing "their."

⟨there being a war then between France and Spain⟩ and possibly might carry us away and set us ashore in England.

The master ⟨also⟩ was a little fearful that it was an *Ostendr* and came to me and told me so. But I persuaded him from it for fear he should set sail for the coast of England again. But I and my Lord *W* went both ashore in the cock boat and went up into the town of *ffeckam* and stayed there all that day to provide horses to go away for Roane. [39] ⟨The vessel proved ⟨afterwards⟩ only a French sloop.⟩

So the next day we got to *Roane* ~~where we at first a good Inne that we went into~~ at a good *Inne* in the Fishmarket ⟨one of the best in the town⟩ ⟨where they⟩ made difficulty to receive us taking us by our clothes to be some thiefs or men that had done some very ill thing. Till Mr. *Sandburne* ⟨for whom I sent⟩ a merchant answered for us. ~~An Inne in the fish market.~~

There was one thing observable. That the ship ⟨which brought us over⟩ had the good fortune ~~to bring me over~~ that the *Winde* turned so happily for her that as soon as I had landed and given him a pass for fear of meeting with some of our *Jerzy* frigates. The ~~wind~~ wind carried her directly for *Poole* so as they did not know that that vessel had ever been upon the coast of France.

We stayed at Roane ~~that day~~ one day to provide us ⟨better⟩ clothes and to give notice to the Queen my mother ⟨who was then at *Paris*⟩ that I was safely arrived. ~~And~~ After which I came safely at to *Paris* and met my mother short of *Paris* with coaches ⟨I⟩ going thither in a hired coach.

Notes referring to the severall pages.[17]
Page [40].

There were 6 brothers of the *Penderells* who knew all the secret. And ⟨as I have learnt since by one of them⟩ that the man in whose house I did change my clothes came to one of them ~~and told them that they might give 1000l~~ about 2 days after and asked where I was and told ~~them~~ him that ~~if they did know~~ they might get 1000l ⟨because there was that sum laid upon my head⟩ if they would tell ⟨where I was⟩. But he was so honest that he ~~would but~~ though he did

[17] These notes begin on p. 41 (p. 40 is blank).

Page [40].

It was Mr. Giffard brought me acquainted with White-Ladyes.

Page [40].

I would not change My Cloath's at any of the Penderells Houses, because I meant to make further use of them, and they might be suspected: But rather chose to doe it in a House where they were not Papists, I neither knowing then nor to this day what the man was at whose House I did it. But the Penderells have since endeavoured to mittigate the business of their being tempted by their Neighbour to discover me. But one of them did certainly declare it to me at that time.*

Page [40].

I did not depend upon finding my Lord Willmot, but sent only to know what was become of him. For he and I had agreed to meete at London at the 3 Cranes in the Vintrey, and to inquire for Will Ashbernham.*

Page [48].

I thinck I stayed 2 dayes at Pitchcroft's, but Father Hurlstone can tell better then I.*

Page [50].

A Poor Old Woman that was gleaning in the Feild cryed out of her owne accord, without any occacion given her, Master, Don't you see a Troop of Horse before you?

Page [56].

I stay'd about 2 dayes at Popes.*

Page [60].

At Trent Mrs. Lane and Lassells went home.

Page [62].

I stay'd some 4 or 5 dayes the first time at Franck Windhams House, and was known to most of his Family.

Page [64].

I could never gett my Lord Willmott to putt on any disguise, he saying that he should looke frightfully in it and therefore did never putt on any.

know then where I was he bid him have a care. For now they should only be hanged for their pains (if they did discover I had been there) because I was gone out of all reach.

Mr. *Giffard* brought me acquainted with White Ladies. I ~~chang~~ would not change my ~~habit~~ clothes in any of the *Penderlls* ~~houses~~ houses because I meant to make 〈further〉 use of them and they might be suspected and therefore chose to change my clothes in a house where they were not papists. The king did not nor doth know what the man was at whose house he changed his clothes. ~~for they deny it since that is their excuse~~ The King says that the *Penderells* have since endeavoured to mitigate that business ~~and say it was nothing~~ of their being tempted to discover him by their neighbour but ~~because~~ the king says that one of them did certainly tell it him then.

Page [41].

He did not depend upon finding my Lord *W* ~~for they~~ but ~~only~~ only to enquire what was become of him. For they had agreed to meet 〈at London〉 at the Three Cranes in the Vintry to enquire for *Wm Ashburnham* ~~there at L~~. [42]

Page [49].

The King thinks he stayed 2 days at Pitchcrofts. But Father *Hurdlestone* can tell better than he.

Page [51].

A poor old woman that was gleaning in the field cried out without any occasion given her but of her own accord. *Sr* dont you see a troop of horse before you.

Page [57].

The King stayed about 2 days at *Popes*.

Page [61].

At *Trent* Mrs. *Lane* and *Lassells* went home.

Page [63].

Stayed some 4 or 5 days the first time at *ffr W*.

Was known to most of his house.

Page [65].

My Lord *W* never put on any disguise. I could not get him, saying that he should look frightfully.[18]

[18] Remainder of this page is blank: four blank pages follow.

Endorsement of the shorthand report

NEWMARKET.

OCTOBER 3, 1680

*A journal of the King's
Escape from Worcester
taken by me this day
in Short-hand from the
King's owne Mouth.*
                    S. Pepys.

NEWMARKET. SUNDAY

OCT. 3. 1680

Notes taken by me SP this day from the King's own mouth in his closet alone at *Newmarket* in the evening, taking up 3 hours—at the instance of his R.H.—touching the whole method of the King's escape after the battle of *Worcester*. Carried this first setting to the end of the second line *Page* 29. And continued to the end in the morning on *Tuesday Oct. 5* in the same closet alone as before. And notes upon the former day's work.

NOTES

The references are to Pepys's own transcription at the places marked by asterisks.

page 38, l. 21, Blount adds these names: Lord Talbot, Col. Edward Roscarrock, Richard Lane, Hugh May, Peter Street, Charles Giffard, "and some others". *Miraculum Basilicon* adds Sir William Armorer.

page 40, l. 1. The town was probably Stourbridge. l. 12. Further details of the happenings at Boscobel and of the activities of the Penderels are given in *An Exact Narrative*. l. 26. This clothing was provided by Richard Penderel: Humphrey P. provided a hat, Edward Martin a shirt, and William Creswell shoes.

page 42, l. 15. Blount says this wood was Spring Coppice, half a mile from White Ladies. l. 22. Judging from Blount's narrative, this may have been Colonel Blundell. Talbot, Buckingham, Blague, and Darcy escaped; but Derby, Lauderdale, Giffard, and some others were captured. Derby was taken to West Chester, tried, and executed on October 15, the day the King escaped to France; Lauderdale and others were imprisoned in the Tower. l. 23. Other versions affirm that William Penderel's wife Margaret brought him food and milk.

page 44, l. 29. Other accounts state that this was Evelin (Evelith) Mill, about two miles from Madeley, and that the miller was actually entertaining royalist soldiers.

page 46, l. 27. According to *An Exact Narrative*, it was a haymow.

page 48, l. 7. According to *An Exact Narrative*, they were guided by Woolfe's maid. l. 19. This was William P., who was housekeeper at Charles Giffard's house at Boscobel. l. 27. The house was Moseley Hall, and the owner's name was actually Thomas Whitgreave—the King somehow confused his name with that of the meadow where the royalist forces mustered before the battle of Worcester.

page 50, l. 8. This was Richard P., who contacted Whitgreave through George Manwaring and Father Huddleston. l. 13. Soon after the King left Moseley, Colonel Careless managed to escape in disguise to Holland. l. 19. Other accounts say that all the brothers went with the King as his guards, armed with clubs and bills, and that Francis Yates and Col. Careless went with them. l. 20. As Huddleston points out, this is a mistake for "mother." l. 22. The happenings at Moseley are told in much fuller detail in Huddleston's and Whitgreave's narratives. l. 26. This was Jane Lane, later Lady Fisher. l. 32. John Penderel attended the King.

page 52, l. 3. The village may have been Bromsgrove, which the King may have confused with Long Marston. l. 14. The name is blank in both shorthand and transcription. The couple were Withy (Lane) and her husband John Petre of Horton, Bucks. l. 17. Blount says that this occurred at Wotton, Warw. l. 37. The name of Mrs. Lane's kinsman was John (Tombs): his wife's name was Amy.

page 54, l. 1. Colloquial form for Cirencester; they stayed at *The Crown*. l. 2. George Norton of Abbots Leigh, three miles from Bristol. Blount says the King went by way of Chipping Sodbury and Bristol. l. 5. John Pope had served at Lichfield under Colonel Bagot, and by that means, according to Blount, had had Charles's looks imprinted in his memory. l. 13. Henry Lascelles, who had served in the Civil War as cornet to Colonel Lane. l. 18. Blount credits Margaret Rider, the Nortons' maid, with taking this particular care of "William Jackson."

page 56, l. 33. The place that was tried was called *Crods and Peet* (Crokenpill?). l. 36. Wilmot had gone from Bentley to Sir Clement Fisher's house at Packington, Warw., and thence to John Winter's at Dirnham, Glocs. His alias at this time was Mr. Morton.

page 58, l. 36. According to Blount, the King stayed with Edward Kirton, who was then steward at Castle Cary for the Marquis of Hertford. l. 39. Some further details about the occurrences at Trent are given by Anne Wyndham in *Claustrum Regale Reseratum* (1667), which is included in the 1680 and later editions of Blount's *Boscobel* (also in Hughes, *Boscobel Tracts* and Fea, *After Worcester Fight*).

page 60, l. 13. Captain Alford and Anne Wyndham say that the sum was one hundred pounds in gold. l. 20. Wyndham's alias for this occasion was "Captain Norris." l. 21. The master's name was Stephen Limbry. l. 25. Her right name was Juliana Coningsby.

page 62, l. 2. Henry Peters (Petre). l. 2. The village was Charmouth; the inn was *The Queens Arms,* kept by Margaret Wade. l. 11. An explanation is given in Gregory Alford's letter; another and quite different explanation is given by Ellesdon himself in an appendix to Alford's account in the present edition. Anne Wyndham gives the same explanation as Ellesdon. l. 14. This is an error for "Bridport." l. 22. They were embarking at Weymouth. l. 24. The inn was *The George.* l. 36. The hostler's name was Henry Hall.

page 64, l. 27. The village was Broad Windsor: this name is added in the shorthand notes in the form "Broad Windorr" but is blank in Pepys's transcription. According to other narratives, the King put up at *The George Inn,* which was kept by Rice Jones.

page 66, l. 3. Fuller details of the remainder of the King's adventures after he left Trent are given in Phillips' and Gounter's narratives. l. 5. The messenger was Wilmot, attended by Henry Peters. l. 9. According to Phillips and Anne Wyndham, John Coventry played a large part in the attempt to get shipping from Southampton, although the King does not mention him. l. 16. Blount says that the King went via Wincanton and Mere, lunching at *The George Inn* at Mere, where the host, Christopher Philips, toasted King Charles.

He also says that at this time the King pretended to be a tenant of Colonel Phillips. l. 27. Humphrey Henchman, at that time Bishop of Salisbury.

page 68, l. 19. Gounter says they met at Warneford, Hants. l. 20. An error for "Hambledon." l. 30. The name, Thomas Symonds, is left blank in both the shorthand and the transcription.

page 70, l. 3. Symonds' suspicion was probably roused by the close haircut that William Penderel had given the King. l. 8. Blount states that Wilmot sought help from various acquaintances, among them, Thomas Henslow of Burhant, who in time sought help of the Earl of Southampton. In the next line the King confuses Henslow with Bishop Henchman apparently. l. 18. The name, Francis Mancell, is left blank in the shorthand notes and transcription. l. 22. The shorthand shows that "at supper" has been accidentally omitted in the transcription: Dalrymple guessed the omission to have been "sitting together," and this has been adopted in later editions. l. 22. Philipps had actually left the party at Hambledon: he went to London to arrange for the bill of exchange which the King later picked up in Rouen. l. 38. According to Gounter, Tattersall did not know who his passengers were, and his behavior was much more mercenary than the King suggests.

page 72, l. 8. The inn was *The George.* Blount and Gounter say the landlord's name was Gaius Smith, formerly one of Charles I's guards. l. 36. The shorthand indicates that "would not stand his course over to France" has been accidently omitted after this word.

page 74, l. 7. One of the sailors was named Thomas Tuppon, the mate was Richard Carver, and the ship's name was *The Surprise.*

page 76, l. 21. Tattersall's boat was after the Restoration taken into the navy as a fifth-rate, named *The Royal Escape,* and anchored in the Thames at Whitehall. l. 22. The King stayed in Rouen at Mr. Scot's. l. 26. The King arrived in Paris on October 30.

page 78, l. 11. Blount says that Humphrey Penderel told the King and Colonel Careless that while he had been at Shefnal on Saturday, September 6, a Cromwellian colonel who was searching for the King had questioned him about the King's whereabouts and told him the penalty for concealment and the reward for discovery. Humphrey had pleaded ignorance, and then retired to Boscobel and told the King and Careless. After the King had left Boscobel, the brothers were all questioned and threatened. On June 13, 1660, the five brothers visited the King at Westminster and were rewarded. l. 16. *Miraculum Basilicon* gives the rendezvous as the *Green Dragon*. l. 19. The King actually stayed three days at Whitgreave's. l. 25. This should be the Nortons' place, Abbots Leigh, where Pope was butler.

ᵥ

AN EXACT NARRATIVE
AND RELATION
(1660)

This narrative is bound in at the end of Pepys's collection concerning the King's flight. It is the only printed item on this subject in his library. It was published by G. Colborn in two London editions in 1660, with the same text but slightly differing titles: (1) *An Exact Narrative and Relation of his Most Sacred Majesties Escape from Worcester on the third of September 1651. Till his Arrivall at Paris;* (2) *A True Narrative and Relation.* The latter is reprinted in Allan Fea's *Flight of the King* (London, 1897); the former, which is the edition Pepys owned, has been reprinted in Volume 5 of *Royal and Loyal Sufferers* (London, 1903).

The narrative, one of several that were published in the year of the King's return, is concerned almost entirely with the first week of Charles's flight, while he was at White Ladies, Boscobel, and Moseley Hall; the events of the other five weeks are summarized in a short paragraph. The emphasis is upon the activities of the Penderel brothers on the King's behalf, and since the detail is at times intimate and the language has traces of local dialect, it is likely that the narrative was based on enquiries made in the Boscobel area and probably on interviews with the Penderels.

It may be assumed that it was this emphasis that led Pepys to select this particular item from the several printed narratives that must have been available to him. His general plan was apparently to support the King's overall narrative with a range of special narratives from persons who gave major help to the King during his flight. It is on that assumption that the item has been transferred in this edition to the chronological position that best suits it—first among the supporting narratives.

THE

KINGS

Escape from *Worcester*.

Fortune had now twice Counterfeited and double-Gilt the Trophees of Rebellion, and its Brazen Trumpet repeated *Victory*, betrayed or prostituted before at *Dunbar*, & now ravished at *Worcester* by numerous over-powring Force, on that Black and White day *September* the 3d. 1651. in the Dusk of which Fatall Evening, when the ashamed Sun had blush't in his setting, and plunged his Affrighted Head into the depth of Lucklesse *Severn*, and the Night ready to Stain and Spot her guilty Sables with loyal Blood, was attiring her self for the Tragedy; The King, whose first and conspicuous valorous Essay so exceeded all comparison that it cannot but oblige Fate to preserve that Matchlesse courage and never again to venture or expose it to any Hazard) compelled to Abandon the City of *Worcester*, (whose Fidelity and Affection deserves perpetual Memory,) after he had quitted his Court and Lodgings to which he retired from the Field, having rallied his most Faithful and Considerable Friends, divers English Lords and Gentlemen, who were resolved to accompany him in his Flight; was presented by that renowned Earle of *Derby* with one *Charles Gifford* Esquire, (a person of note then of that Country and of much manifested Honour since to the World) to be his Majesties Conductor in this Miraculous, blessed Escape: who forthwith called for one *Francis Yates*, whom he had brought with him under the Command of Colonel *Carelesse* in a party that met the KING in his Advance to

CHARLES II, *ca.* 1651
Portrait by Philippe de Champaigne

SAMUEL PEPYS, *ca.* 1680
Portrait by Sir Godfrey Kneller

CHARLES II, *ca.* 1680

THE FIRST PAGE OF PEPYS'S SHORTHAND NOTES
OF THE KING'S OWN STORY

PEPYS'S ADDITIONAL NOTES ON THE KING'S OWN STORY

Father Huddlestone.

A Brief Account of his Maties
Escape from Worcester. And
of his happie Preservation
& the first seaven daies after
& that unfortunate Defeate
Wednesday Septemb: 3.
1651.

Charls the 2. By the Grace of God King of
England, Scotland, &c: After his unfortunate
Defeat at Worcester Wednesday Septemb: 3: 1651.
with the Duke of Buckingham, Earl of Derby,
Earl of Landerdaile, Lord Talbot, Lord Wilmot,
Coll: Duke Darcy and others, was that night
by Coll: Charls Gifford conducted safe to white
Ladies

Thursday morning
—there presently disguised, and privately conveyed
into the woods by Richard Pendrell alone, his
Nobility and Traine then dispersing themselves
Lord Wilmot (as himself related) apprehending
the London Roade his likelyest way to escape
took John Pendrell to guide him therinto and
his servant there into. Thereupon the news of
his Maties defeate finding the Country so Alarmed,
all waies so strictly guarded with Soldiers but
especially

THE FIRST PAGE OF FATHER HUDDLESTONE'S REPORT

Coll. Phillipps Notes.

On Thursday ye 2d of September 1651, The then Ld Wilmott (afterward Earle of Rochester) was sent by his Matie from Trent in Somersetshire, ye house of Coll. Francis Wyndham, to Salisbury, to Mr Coventrye and Coll: Robert Phelips which was occasioned by Mr Edward Hyde (brother in law to Coll: Francis Wyndham) discourse there at Dinner of ye day before, who said yt he had been at Salisbury where he saw his father Phelips (for soe he usually called him) returned to his family, and yt he was permitted by ye Committee to remaine for, ye unfortunate businesse of Worcester having at present quieted their feares and jealousies. My Ld at his arrivall to ye Kings armes Inn, then kept by a hearty Cavaleere Mr Henry Hewitt sent first to Mr John Coventrye to whom my Lord discoursed his errand; and then Mr Coventrye sent for Coll Phelips who presently came, and after my Ld and he had saluted (they having bin formerly acquainted) in ye armie Mr Coventrye left ym together saying he would goe into ye next roome and take a pipe of tobaco with Mr Hewitt: Then my Ld asked ye Coll whether hee could helpe a gentleman in distresse out of ye Kingdome ye Coll answered, he would willingly give him ye best directions he could; it being ye duty every gentleman owed another in such circumstances, but was reserved enough, (having heard before, yt ye Ld had too warmly ingaged himselfe with Argyles faction in Scotland) wch ye Ld quickly perceiving, told him, Sr I am commanded to be free with you, and to let you know yt ye King is at Coll Wyndhams house at Trent and his condition is such, yt he knows not how to dispose of himselfe; he is assured of yor fidelitie, and is told, yt noe man is more capable to serue him in this exigent, he therefore committs himselfe to yor care, to provide for his safety; at wch discourse ye Coll was not a little amazed, and could not undertake soe difficult a province without great apprehensions of what might not only possibly, but even probably (as things then stood) unfortunately fall out; but then on ye other hand considering yt it was a riske which he venturd on; or then on yt if he would undertake it, assuring him yt if ye King ye King he lost; he told yt if ye Ld he would undertake it, and ye willing sacrificing of his owne life should beare miscarried in his hands, ye willing sacrificing of his owne life should beare testimonie of his truth and sinceritie; then came in Mr Coventry and said well gentlemen are you agreed, both answered yes; then after drinking a bottle or two of wine and discourse of their adventures since Worcester fight Mr Coventry and ye Coll tooke theire leaves; and as they went along ye Coll ye Coll acquainted Mr Coventrye with what had past betweene ye Lord and him; and Mr Coventry was glad yt ye Coll had undertaken it, and wished him good lucke, assuring him yt he would assist in any thing within his power soe they parted to their severall homes; and ye next morning early ye Coll: went to Southampton to one Mr Horne a marchent of very good credit in that towne and a very good acquaintance of ye Colls but he being out of towne, and intending to returne home ye next day ye Coll left a little for him importing yt he had earnest businesse to speake with him; and yt he was only gon to Coll: St Barbs

THE FIRST PAGE OF COLONEL PHILLIPS'S REPORT

Upper, WHITELADIES   *Lower,* ABBOTS LEIGH

(Both from *Flight of the King* by ALLAN FEA)

Worcester, to be guide-assistant for the surer finding the byways for his Majesties speed and safety.

In the mean time Colonel *Carelesse* (a Gentleman of very Gallant and Noble Endowments) was commanded to sustain the Brunt of the pursuing Enemy, and to keep them off while the KING might be somewhat in his way; which with excellent Prudence and Valour he did to effect, and afterwards fled to his old retract and coverture, passing by *Hartlebury* Castle, then Garrisond by the Enemy, whom he Couragiously Fought with and broke through, and came safe to his Designed shelter.

Towards three a Clock *Thursday* morning the 4 of *September*, the KING in company with the said Earle of *Derby*, Earle of *Shrewsbury*, Earle of *Cleaveland*, Duke of *Buckingham*, my Lord *Wilmot*, and others to the number of Fourscor came to the place called *White-Ladies* in the Parish of *Tong* in the confines of *Stafford* and *Shropshire*, being 25 miles distant or there abouts from *Worcester*, which space of ground he had rid that night.

This *White-Ladies* was a house belonging to one *Fitz Harbert*, where one *George Pendril* (the youngest Brother of the five who were all severally instrumental in the conductment and preservation of his Majesty) hearing somebody knocking at the Gate so early, opening the Window he espied there the aforesaid *Francis Yates*, who was his brother in Law, with Mr. *Gifford*; to whom he presently opened the door, and enquired of his brother *Yates* what News from *Worcester*, who told him that the KING was Defeated and in Pursuite, and therefore bid him to make hast and put on his Cloaths. But before he could make himself ready, the King with most of his Lords had entred the house, and came into the Hall, where after a short consultation held among them, the Earle of *Derby* called for *William Pendrill* the Eldest brother, (you must know that my Lord of *Derby* had taken this place for a subterfuge, after the defeat given him by Colonel *Lilburn* neer *Wigan* in *Lanchashire*, and was acquainted there, and by them conveyed to *Worcester* to the King; as also several other Gentlemen before had used this for their Sanctuary) who being come, *George* was sent to *Tong* to one *Robert Beard* an Honest Subject to enquire of him whether there were any scattered parties of the Kings thereabouts, or any of the Enemies appearing; who brought word that the Coast was yet clear and no parties at all to be seen. In his return he met with his Brother *Richard*; for now those few Inhabitants that Lived there, were awakened with the Noyse, and their own ill boding thoughts and fears of the successe at *Worcester.*

Richard was no sooner come in, but Squire *Gifford* called for him, and bad him make hast, and bring with him his best Cloaths, which were a Jump and Breeches of Green course Cloth and a Doe skin Leather Doublet, the Hat was borrowed of *Humphrey Pendrill* the Miller being an old Gray one that turned up its Brims—the Shirt (which in that Countrey Language they call'd an Hurden or Noggen Shirt, of Cloath that is made of the coursest of the Hemp,) was had of one *Edward Martin*, *George Pendrills* Bond, and *William Creswells* Shoos; which the King having presently unstripped himself of his own Cloaths, did nimbly d'on. His Buffe Coat, and Linnen Doublet, and a Gray pair of Breeches which he wore before, he gave into these Brothers Hands, who forthwith buried them underground, where they lay five weeks, before they durst take them up again. The Jewels off his Arm he gave to one of the Lords then departing.

Then *Richard* came with a pair of Shears and rounded the King's hair, which my Lord *Wilmot* having cut before with a Knife, had untowardly notched; and the King was pleased to take notice of *Richard's* good barbing, so as to prefer his work before my Lord *Wilmots*, and gave him the praise of it; and now his Majesty was *A la mode* the Woodman.

Hereupon *William Pendril* was brought to the King by the Earl of *Derby*, and the care and preservation of his most sacred Majesty committed to his charge and the rest of the Brothers, (my Lord would have staid too but there was no undertaking security for them both) and presently the Lords took their heavy leave and departed, every one shifting for himself. Onely my Lord *Wilmot* was conveyed by *John Pendrill* to Mr. *Thomas Whitgreaves*, but he would have left him at several other places wich my Lord did in no wise approve of; first at one *John Shores* of *Hungerhill*, thence to *John Climpson*, then to one *Reynolds* of the *Hide*, so to *John Hunspatches*, where passing by *Coven*, they had notice of a Troop of Horse in the Town, and seeing some men coming behind them, (which proved to be Friends, though my Lord suspected the Country rise upon them) they betooke themselves into a dry pit, where they stayed till Evening, and then arrived safely at Mr. *Whitgreaves.*

The Company being all departed, a Wood-bill was brought, and put into the Kings hand, and he went out with *Richard* into the adjoining Woods. *William* departed home, and *Humphrey* and *George* went out to scout, and lay hovering in the Woods to hear or see if any one approached that way. But the King had not been an hour in the Wood, before a Troop of Horse of the Enemies came to *Whit-ladies,* and enquired, if some of the Kings Horse and himself passed not that way, and if they could give any Information of him; to which the Townes-folks answered, that about 3 hours ago there was a Party of Horse came thither, and they supposed the King with them, but they made no stay in the Village, but presently departed; they were hereupon so eager in the pursuit that after enquiring which way they took, they followed the rout, and made no further search there. The King straight heard this by the two aforesaid Scouts, who stragled for Intelligence into the Town.

All this day, being *Thursday,* the King continued in the Wood upon the ground, *Richard Pendrill* being constantly with him, and sometimes the other two Brothers: It proved to be a very rainy day, and the King was wet with showers, thereupon *Francis Yates* his wife came into the Wood and brought the King a Blanket, which she threw over his shoulders, to keep him dry; she also brought him his first meat he eat there, *viz.* a Messe of Milk, Eggs and Sugar in a black earthen Cup, which the King guessed to be Milk and Apples, and said, he loved it very well; after he had drank some of it and eaten part in a pewter Spoon, he gave the rest to *George* and bid him eat; for it was very good. There was nothing of moment passed this day in Court but only the King exchanged his Wood bill for *Francis Yates* Broom *hook,* which was something lighter.

They had much adoe all that day to teach and fashion his Majesty to their Country guise, and to order his steps and straight body to a lobbing, jobsons gate, and were forced every foot to mind him of it; for the Language, his Majesties most gracious converse with his People in his Journey to, and at *Worcester,* had rendred it very easie and very tunable to him.

About 5. a clock that Evening, the King with the retinue

of *Richard, Humphrey, George,* and *Francis Yates* left the wood, and betook himself to *Richards* house, where he went under the name of *William Jones,* a woodcutter newly come thither for work; against his coming, the good wife for his entertainment at supper, was preparing a *Fricasse* of Bacon and Eggs, and while that was doing, the King held on his knee their daughter *Nan:* after he had eat a little, he asked *Richard* to eat, who replied, yea Sir I will, whereto His Majesty answered, you have a better stomach then I, for you have eaten five times to day already. After supper ended, the King according to his resolution to passe into *Wales,* prepared (when it should be dusky) to depart; before he went, *Jane Pendryll* the Mother of the five Brethren, came to see the King, before whom she blessed God that had so honoured her Children in making them the instruments (as she hoped) of his Majesties safeguard and deliverance. Here *Francis Yates* offered the King thirty shillings in silver, the King accepted ten, and bad him put the other up. *Humphrey* would have gone before to see and view about, but the King would not let him; it being now near night, they took their leave of the King upon their knees, beseeching God to guide and blesse him.

So the King and *Richard* only, departed to go to one Mr. *Francis Wolfe* of *Madeley,* there to take passage into *Wales.* On the way they were to passe by a Mill, at a place called *Evelin,* and going over ('twas about nine a clock at night) the bridge of the said Mill, the Milner steps forth, and demanded, who goes there? having a quarterstaffe or a good cudgel in his hand, to which *Richard* being formost thought it not safe to reply, but the water being shallow, leapt of the bridge into it, and the King did the like, following *Richard* by the noyse and ratling of his leather breeches; the Milner being glad he was so rid of them; for (as it afterwards appeared) here was some of the King's scattered Souldiers in his Mill, and he supposed the other to be *Parliamentarians* that were upon the scent for his distressed guests.

Being come to *Madely* to the said Master *Francis Wolfes* late that Night, they understood there was no passage over the water into *Wales,* and that it was very dangerous to abide there, the Countrey being every where about laid with souldiers, nor durst he entertain them into his House, but shewed them a Haymow where they might lodge; and there the King and

Richard continued all that night, and the next day being *Friday*, and that night with the conveyance of a Maid of this Master *Wolfes*, who brought the King two miles on his way, they retreated back again to *Richards* House: Mr. Wolfe lent the King some small sum of money.

This design being crossed, *Saturday* morning without any stay at *Richards*, the King and he went to a House of Mistris *Giffards*, called *Boscabell*, where *William Pendril* and his wife dwelt as House-keepers for the said *Giffard*, who received him joyfully; but the Kings feet were so blistered with travelling in such course and stiffe accoutrements as he wore on his feet, and lying in them, that he was scarce able to stand or go, which *Williams* wife perceiving, she stript off his stockins and cut the blisters, and washed his feet, and gave the King some Ease.

The same time or near thereupon, that Noble Colonel *Carelesse*, who as is said before made good the Kings Rear at *Worcester*, and had fought his way through, after he had been two dayes at one *David Jones* living in the *Heath* in *Tong-Parish*, and there by him secured, (for this Col. had lain 3 quarters of a year before obscured in this Countrey, when he had been narrowly every where searcht after) was brought by one *Elizabeth Burgesse* to this same House of *Boscabell;* and there His Majesty and he met, but the Col. was so overjoyed with the sight of the King his Master in such sure and safe hands, that he could not refrain weeping, and the King was himself something moved with the same passion.

After a short conference and but inchoated councel of the Kings probablest means of escape, it was resolved by them to betake themselves to the wood again; and accordingly about nine of the clock that *Saturday* morning the 6. of *September* they went into the wood, and Col. *Carelesse* brought and led the King to that so much celebrated Oake, where before he had himself been lodged: (This Tree is not hollow but of a sound firm Trunk, onely about the middle of the body of it there is a hole in it about the bignesse of a mans head, from whence it absurdly and abusively (in respect of its deserved perpetual growth to outlast Time it self) is called Hollow; and by the help of *William Pendrils* wood-ladder they got up into the boughs and branches of the Tree, which were very thick and well spread, and full of leaves; so that it was impossible for any one to discerne through them.

When they were both up, *William* gave them up two pillows to ly upon between the thickest of the branches, and the King being overwearied with his travel and sore journey, began to be very sleepy; The Col. to accommodate him the best he could, desired his Majesty to lay his head in his lap, and rest the other parts of his body upon the pillow, which the King did; and after he had taken a good nap, (*William,* and his wife *Joane* still peaking up and down, and she commonly near the place with a nutt-hook in her hand gathering of sticks) awaked very hungry, and wished he had something to eat: whereupon the Col. pluckt out of his pocket a good lunchion of bread and cheese, which *Joane Pendrill* had given him for provant for that day, and had wrapt it up in a clean linnen cloth, of which the King fed very heartily, and was well pleased with the service, and commended highly his good chear; and some other smal relief he had, which was put up into the Tree with a long hook-stick.

In the mean while *Richard Pendrill* (the first Esquire) was sent to *Woller-Hampton* some three miles thence being a Market Town, to buy Wine and Bisket, and some other necessary refreshments for the King; and withal to speak with one Mr. *George Manwaring,* a person of known Integrity and Loyalty from Col. *Carelesse,* with some instructions about the Kings removal, though not expresly the King, but one of that ruined Party: in effect it was to know of him, whether he knew of any sure privacy for 2 such persons: to which he answered that he had not himself, but would enquire if a friend of his, one Master *Whitgreave* of *Moseley* (formerly and again to be spoken of here) could do it. (So that we may see what a Loyal honest combination and secrecy there was between all of these persons;) and then *Richard* returned with his Wine, &c. to the King; who towards the Evening came down by the same ladder from the Tree, and was brought into the Garden of *Boscable* House, where he sate in the Bower of it, and dranke part of the Wine till toward night.

Neither was *Humphrey Pendrill* the Miller un-employed all this while, but was sent to get intelligence how things went.

And the easilier to come by it, he was sent to a Captain of the *Rump* one *Broadways,* formerly a Heelmaker, under pretence of carrying him twenty shillings for the pay of a man in the new raised *Militia* of their County for their Mistres. While he was there in came a Colonel of the *Rebels,* and asked for Captain *Broadway,* on purpose to know what further enquiry had been made at *White-Ladies* for the King, relating to *Broadway* the Story of it; to which he replyed he knew nothing of it further then rumour, but that there was one of that place in the House that could give him an account of it. So *Humphrey* was called, and several questions put to him, which he evaded, but confest that the King had been there as was supposed, but there was no likelyhood for him to stay there, for there was three Families in the House, and all at difference with one another. The Col. told him there was a thousand pound offered to any that would take or discover him, and that they doubted not, but within a day or two to have him delivered into their hands.

These tydings *Humphrey* brought with him, and omitted not to tell his Majesty of the price his Rebells had set on him; at the telling of which, the King looked something dismayed, as having trusted his Life into the hands of such poor Men, whom such a summe as that, (though both detestable, and of inconsiderable value to the Purchase) might pervert from their Allegiance and Fidelity: which made *Humphrey* to be exceedingly troubled for his rashness, while Collonel *Carelesse* assured the King, if it were 100000 *l.* it were to no more purpose, and that he would engage his Soul for their truth; which *Humphrey* also with many urgent asseverations did second.

It was late, and the King was very hungry, and had a minde to a Loyn of Mutton, and being come into the House, asked *William* if he could not get him such a Joynt, to which he replyed, that he had it not of his own, but he would make bold at that time, and for that occasion, with one of his Masters Sheep in the Cote; which instantly he did, and brought it into the ground Cellar; where the Collonel not having the patience to stay while he fetcht a Knife, stabb'd it with his Dagger; and when *William* came down they hung it upon a door, and *fleyd* it, and brought up a hind Quarter to the King, who presently fell a chopping of the Line to pieces, or (as they called it then) into Scotch Collops, which the Collonel clapt into the Pan while the King held it and fryed it.[1]

This passage yeilded the King a pleasant jocular discourse, after his Arrival in *France,* when it amounted to a Question, (a very difficult case) who was Cook, and who was Scullion? and for solution of the doubt, when it could not be decided by the Lords then present, was referred to the judgement of his Majesties Master Cook, who affirmed that the King was *hic & nunc,* both of them.

When this nimble Collation was ended, it was time for the King to betake himself to his rest, and his Chamberlain *William* brought him to his appartiment. It was a place made between two Walls, on purpose for secrecy, contrived at the building of the House; thither they let the King down, where he slept very incommodiously with little or no rest, for that the place was not long enough for him, and therefore the next night they laid him a sorry Bed upon the Stair-case, as they used to do for strange Woodcutters, that the meannesse of his lodging might secure him from suspicion.

My Lord *Wilmot* as is said before, was all this while safe at Master *Whitgreaves,* onely his care of the King made him full of trouble. His hiding place was so sure a one, that at his first coming to it, he wished so he gave 20000 *l.* that the King were either as secure, or there with him; he therefore dispatched away *John Pendrill* (who had attended him all along) to the *White Ladies,* to enquire for the King, and to give him notice of the conveniency that was at Master *Whitegreaves;* but when he came thither, which was on Friday, the King was then gone to *Madeley,* to Master *Wolfes.* The next day he was sent againe, and by *Richards* Wife directed to *Boscabel,* where he delivered the King the Message, which the King assented unto, and resolved to remove thither.

Munday night, *September* 8 [2]. at eleven at night, was the time appointed for the Kings progresse to *Moseley,* but a Horse

[1] Blount says the sheep belonged to William Staunton, who rented some of the demesnes of Boscobel. After the King had gone, Penderel tried to repay Staunton, who loyally refused payment however.

[2] Here, and subsequently, this document reports events a day later than other accounts.

was hard to be found. *John* was ordered to borrow one of one *Stanton* of *Hatton,* but he had lent his out before; when the Collonel remembered that *Humphrey* the Miller had one, and he thereupon was called and desired to lend him for the Kings Service; it was a kinde of War-horse, that had carryed many a load of provision, Meal and such like, but now he put upon him a Bridle and Saddle, that had out-worn its Tree and Irons, and at the time prefixed brought him to the Gate.

As soon as the King had notice of it, out he came, and would have had none but Collonel *Carelesse,* and *John* to have gone along with him, but they told him, it was very dangerous to venture himselfe with so few, they therefore intreated his Majesty that he would give them leave to go with him, which at their importunity he granted.

Having mounted the King, Collonel *Carelesse* and the six brethren guarding him, two before, and two behinde, and one of each side, armed with Clubs and Bills (*Humphrey,* leading his Horse by the Bridle) they began their journey. It was five miles from *Boscabel* to *Mosely* Master *Whitgreaves,* and the way in some places miry, where the Horse blundering, caused the King to suspect falling, and bid *Humphrey* have a care, to which he answered, that that now fortunate Horse had carried many a heavier weight in his time, six strike of Corn (which measure the King understood not) but now had a better price on his back, the price of three Kingdomes, and therefore would not now shame his Master.

Their travel was soon and safe ended, and the King brought the back way to a stile that led to the House, *Humphries* led the Horse into a Ditch, and the King alighted off upon the stile; but forgetting that most of his Guard were to return home, was gone five or six steps onward, without taking leave of them, but recalling himself returned back and said, I am troubled that I forget to take my leave of my friends; but if ever I come into *England* by fair or foul means, I will remember you, and let me see you when ever it shall so please God; so they all kissed his Hand and departed, but the Collonel, *John,* and *Francis Yates,* who guided the King to the House.

There Master *Thomas Whitgreave* received the King dutifully and affectionately, and brought him in to my Lord

Wilmot, who with infinite gladnesse, kneeled down and embraced his knees. After a little conference, his Majesty was had to his lodging, and the intriques of it shown him; where after the King had rested himselfe that night, they entred into consultation about the escape, which had been projected by my Lord *Wilmot* before.

Francis Yates departed, but *John* staid two or three dayes longer with the King, while he went away. On Wednesday noon a Troop of the Rebels horse passed through the Town and made no stay, which *John* told not the King of till after noon, because (as he then said) he would not spoil his Majesties Dinner.

Now the King prepared and fitted himself for his journey, and one Mr. *Huddlestone* and Master *Whitgreave* accommodated him with Boots, Cloak, Money, &c. and *John Pendril* was sent to Mistresse *Lane* about it, who sent him back again with a parcel of leaves of Walnuts, boyled in Spring Water, to colour his Majesties hands, and alter the hue and whitenesse of his Skin in those places that were most obvious to the eye, and by him gave notice to the King, what time she should be ready.

On Thursday night the eleventh of *September,* Collonel *Lane* came with his Sister to a field adjoyning, and there they put the King before her. *John* having the honour to hold the Kings Stirrup while he mounted, and presently they two set forward, (having taken directions to know the Countrey) and my Lady *Lane* having several recommendations to the allyes, friends and acquaintance of her family, that lay in their intended road, if any untoward occasion should put them to the tryal.

The several adventures which that Heroical Lady passed and overcame, in the management of that grand affair of his Majestyes life, will become and befit a worthier Paper, and a Nobler Pen, and therefore let the blessed and thrice happy event of that her fortunate Loyalty, restrain a curious enquiry of the means, which probably may be some *arcana imperii,* secrecy of State now, as well as then of the King, not yet fit to be divulged. Miracles indeed of this benigne and propitious influence are very rare (God hath not dealt so with the Nations round about us) Especially where Humane Coadjument, and that so signally (in the tacitenesse of so many persons concerned) hath been instrumental; and therefore why may we not (as we fearfully behold

Comets) with delight look upon the serene smiles of Heaven (in His Majesties preservation) and the Rayes of its Goodnesse diffused into the Breasts of those Loyal Persons his Guardians, (for whose Honour more especially this Paper officiously obtrudes it self) with such weak eyes as we now see with, before we can have the benefit of a prospective (the full Relation)

Let it therefore suffice and content us, that it pleased the Divine Wisedome and Goodness to protect and defend our most gracious Soveraign in all dangers and places and conditions whatsoever, in that his incumbred passage through his own rightful Dominions, and without the least umbrage of suspition, to conveigh him out of the hands of his blood-thirsty Trayterous Enemies, who thought themselves sure of Him, *That so killing the Heir, the Inheritance might be theirs.*

He remained or rather Pilgrimaged from one Sanctuary to another in *England* near the space of five weeks, and like other Princes, though not on the same Account was present *incognito* while such time as a Convenience of Passage could be found for him in *Sussex*, where after he had Embarqued Himself in a Barke out of a Creek, He was put back again by contrary weather into the same place, being disguised in a *Saylors cloaths*; but the wind veering about more favourably about the end of *October,* 1651. Landed at *Deep* in *Normandy*, from whence an Expresse was sent to her Majesty of *England,* to acquaint her of His safe Arrival, which was presented communicated to the *French* Court, who appearingly with great Manifestation of Joy welcomed the Newes: But His Majesties most Affectionate Uncle, the late Duke of *Orleans* did with entire joy, As also sundry of the most eminent *French* Nobility, Congratulate His Deliverance, which they testified by a most Splendid and Honourable *Cavalcade* at His Reception and Entry into *PARIS*.

FINIS

~VI~

A LETTER
FROM THE LADY TUKE

On May 21, 1681, the Duke of York wrote to Pepys asking him to send a transcript of the King's narrative and promising that no further copy would be taken of it. Pepys replied on June 4, explaining that

> . . . my covetousness of rendr'ing it as perfect, as the memory of any of the Survivers (interested in any part of that memorable Story) can enable me to make it, has ledde me into so many & distant enquirys relateing thereto, as have kept me out of a capacity of putting it together as I would, & it ought, & shall be, so soon as ever I can possess myselfe of all the Memorialls I am in expectacion of concerning it. Which I shall also (for Your R. H's satisfaccion) use my outmost industry in the hastning.

In the meantime Pepys sent the required transcript, together with a considerable addition that he had since obtained in writing from Colonel Phillips, "suitable to what I am promis'd & daily look for from Father Hurleston."

Evidence of the kind of distant enquiry that Pepys made is afforded by this holograph letter from Lady Mary Tuke, which is here printed for the first time. Lady Mary was the intermediary with Father Huddleston and Thomas Whitgreave; her letter must have been written in 1682, nine months after Pepys reported to the Duke of York his expectation of soon receiving the promised story from Father

Huddleston. Lady Mary transmits this document, asking Pepys to improve its style and to send her a copy when it is put into print. The document therefore witnesses to the difficulties of collecting the material and to the expectation of the contributors that their material would be style-edited and published.

Newmarket, the 13 of March
LADY TUKE TO MR. PEPYS

T he enclosed is what you expect from me, and when you have drest it up with some little additions of your owne, you will doe the Gentilman wright, that indends as well as any body tho' hee has not the talent of writeing soe well, therefore you are free to mend what you please, without feare of disobligin the party, who desires nothing more then to have it well don, and pretends for his part only to furnish you with notes: if you think it necessary to sent a Coppie to Mr. Whitgrave, hee will doe it as soon as hee can, but from this place hee finds it a very difficult matter, and can not, I see,[1] tell how to goe about it till hee comes to London. Lett me know if you desire to have it don out of hand, and wee will contrive some meanes to send it, for my owne part, I beg you will remember me when it is printed and bestoe one uppon

Your humble Servant,

Mary Tuke

[1] Replacing "find."

~VII~
FATHER HUDDLESTON'S
ORIGINAL ACCOUNT

This document is in two sections. The first consists of the notes, apparently in Father Huddleston's own very shaky hand, which Lady Mary Tuke sent to Pepys from Newmarket on March 13, 1682. Lady Tuke had noted that the writer "has not the talent of writeing soe well" and pretended only to furnish notes which Pepys was free to amend as he pleased. The narrative is in the third person, and the manuscript is rough and altered, with some passages in draft style. There are no indications that Pepys has amended the manuscript. The second section consists of "Notes from Father Hurlston," which correct some statements in the King's own narrative and add further details. The first part is in a clerk's hand, with a few alterations in Huddleston's; the last third is in Pepys's own hand. The form is largely question-and-answer, and some of the phraseology indicates that the notes are the product of an interview.

Pepys's procedure seems, therefore, to have been as follows: Having received Huddleston's story from Lady Tuke, he interviewed Huddleston on some discrepancies between his story and the King's and on certain points of detail in which he was interested. He may have shown Huddleston a transcript of the King's own narrative and taken down his comments in shorthand. Part of these notes were then put into a clean copy, which was shown to Huddleston, and partly amended; the rest Pepys later added himself. The procedure is complex and time-consuming, and it witnesses to Pepys's characteristic zeal for getting facts straight and complete.

Except for a few sentences that Dalrymple used as notes in his

1766 edition of the King's narrative, neither Huddleston's narrative nor the appended notes has been printed before. In 1688, however, there was published, "A Summary of Occurrences relating to the miraculous Preservation of our late Sovereign Lord King Charles II after the defeat of his army at Worcester in the year 1651." The pamphlet was issued by the King's Printer, Henry Hills, on behalf of his Household and Chapel; and it was said to be "Faithfully taken from the express Personal Testimony of those two worthy Roman Catholics, Thomas Whitgrave of Moseley in the County of Stafford, Esq., and Mr. John Huddleston, Priest of the Holy Order of St. Bennet, the eminent Instrument under God of the same Preservation. *Permissu Superiorum.*" This document, which was reprinted in *The English Catholic Library* (London, 1884), and in Allan Fea's *The Flight of the King* (London, 1897), is a third person narrative which treats Whitgreave and Huddleston as a single unit. It is very much a Catholic publication, and its arrangement and exposition differ from those in the direct reports that were made by the two men. Even so, it is probable that these may have been the bases from which this propagandist report was composed.

The documents relate to the first week of the King's escape, and mainly to his stay with Thomas Whitgreave at Moseley Hall.

FATHER HUDDLESTONE[1]

A Brief Account of his Majesties Escape from Worcester. And of his happie Preservation the first seaven daies after that unfortunate Defeate, Wednesday, September 3, 1651.

Charles the 2, by the grace of God King of England, Scotland &c., after his unfortunate defeat at Worcester, Wednesday September 3, 1651, with the Duke of Buckingham, Earl of Derby, Earl of Lauderdaile, Lord Talbot, Lord Wilmot, Coll. Duke Darcy, and others, was that night by Coll. Charls Jefford conducted safe to White-Ladies.

Thursday morning. There presently disguised, and privately conveyed into the woods by Richard Pendrell alone, his

---

[1] This ascription is in the hand of the compiler of the table of Contents.

nobility and traine then dispersing themselves, Lord Wilmot (as himself related) apprehending the London Roade his likelyest way to escape, took John Pendrell to guide him and [2] his servant thereinto. They (upon the news of his Majesties defeat) findeing the Countrey so alarm'd, all waies so strictly guarded with soldiers, but especially at severall passages, having had such narrow escapes, and seeing no possibility of passing any further with safety, were glad to withdraw and shelter themselvs in the house of one Mr. Huntbatch of Brinford, where John was obliged to leave the Lord and his servant exposed to what events or injuries might happen them, having their their horses to convey, which he [took] to an obscure, neglected poor cotage thereby: [3] then went to try if possibly hee could finde out any place of more safety for his Lordship among his friends ther about. But being disappointed at all hands, and forced to return, as he passed North-Cote, a countrey farmer's house twixt Bishberry and Moseley, he observed the good woman [4] in her garden as he passed, addressed himself to her, told her his errand over the pales of her garden; which having heard, shee dismissed him forthwith, not daring to give him any encouragement at all in the absence of her husband and disturbance of the countrey.

They parting (as Providence had disposed), one Mr. Hodleston, a stranger in that countrey, then a sejourner with Mr. Thomas Whitgreave at Mosely, a person whom John Pendrell had often seen at White-Ladies, knew well his quality, his loyalty and integrity to his Majestie, passing by them in that moment of time, John leavs the woman, hastens after Mr. Hodleston, asks him if he had not heard yesterdaies sad news, the unfortunate defeat of his Majesties army at Worcester. Mr. Hodleston (not knowing the man, nor much regarding what he said) asked him whence he came and where he had got that bad news. He said at White-Ladies, whence he came that morning and wher that news was well known to be true, as it was bad. And said further: "if I did not know you better then you seem to know me, I should not have been thus bold, for I had commands and cautions sufficient

---

[2] Replacing "there into."
[3] According to Blount, John Penderel left Wilmot in the care of William Walker and sheltered the horses in John Evans' barn.
[4] Blount says this was Mrs. Underhill.

to be circumspect, both what and to whom I spoke. I know you right well, for I have seen you very often with your good friend, my old maister, Mr. Walker, at White-Ladies, whom I left this morning in great trouble to see His Majestie and his friends in that sad and desparate condition—one wherof I have brought to a very near neighboure of yours, a person of quality I belieeve, for hee's a very brave gentleman. There I have left him exposed to all dangers; been at Wolverhampton, in hopes among friends thereabout to have found som place of more safety for him, but am disappointed at all and now going back to see how God hath disposed of him, for if he be not removed this night, he cannot escape." This was the effect of John's discourse to Mr. Hodleston as they passed over [5] the field from North-Cote to Moseley; then, coming to the towns-end, Mr. Hodleston wished John to forbear till they got to his chamber; he would hear him out there.

Mr. Hodleston, having got John to his chamber with what privacy he could, left him there, and desired his patience till he could finde out Mr. Whitgreeve, maister of the house (who was abrode), and he should see what help was possible to be made should not be neglected. Mr. Hodleston, having found Mr. Whitgreeve in the fields, acquainted him with what he had then heard from John, and prevailed with him also to goe along with John to his neighbour Mr. Huntbatch his house, to know the truith and certeinty of the busines and see if there would be need of our help. Which he did forthwith, and had present access to my Lord: who, in brief, told Mr. Whitgreeve into what straits His Majestie and his friends were reduced, what strange escapes he had already made himself in riding those very few miles, and how desperate his own condition was at present in that place, not knowing at all which way to move or what course to steer.

Therupon Mr. Whitegreeve, without more words, resolved with himself to take my Lord to his house; and ordered that about 10 of the clock that night, Mr. Huntbatch should bring his guest into a close of Mr. Whitgreevs in the mid-way; where Mr. Whitgreve, having [6] first ordered his family and seen all his servants at rest, attended his Lordship, who came at the hower

[5] Replacing "from."

[6] Replacing "would attend them at the hower appointed, which he."

place appointed [7] and then Mr. Hunt-batch took his leave of my
Lord, and Mr. Whitgreeve conducted his Lordship [8] with his
servant and necessaries to his house, Mr. Hodlestone in his
chamber expecting Mr. Whitgreevs return. My Lord, after he had
eaten, was willing to rest, but would not unapparrell himself but
only take his repose upon the bed, as he did always, his servant on
a pallat in the same chamber. The necessaries they used not were
secured in the Secret.[9] Their horses that night stood where they
were left by John Pendrell.

Friday morning, very early, Mr. Whitgreve sent Will
Walker, a trusty poor neighbour of his, to [10] Coll. Lane's, to see if
he would entertain two horses of the King's friends, whose
persons he could better secure then them, his stable lying so open
to all that passed. Which the Collonel approved of, and the horses
were sent accordingly and word [brought] back by the same
messenger that the Collonel himself that night would wait upon
the party—and wished Mr. Whitgreve to be ready to receave him
about one of the clock in such a corner of the close next his
house. Which he did, and conducted the Collonel to my Lord;
whom the Collonel (after som discourse) invited to his house, as
a place of more security, and where he might have the benefit of a
pass which his sister had obteined for herself and servants into the
West, if his Lordship approved of that way. His Lordship
returnd thanks; then said, at present he was resolved not to stirr.
And so the Collonel took leave.

That afternoon, my Lord had sent John Pendrell to
White-Ladies to learn how all had passed there with the King—
where John understood that his Majestie, the night before, went
thence with Richard Pendrell towards Wales—with which message John returnd that night, but after the Collonel was gone.
Wherewith my Lord being satisfyed, then resolved to make use of
Mistris Lane's pass for himself; and next morning, being Saturday, sent John to the Collonel to send him his horses that night to
com upon them to him and then dismissed John Pendrell
home.

[7] Replacing "and to."
[8] Replacing "him."
[9] i.e., hiding-place, priest-hole.
[10] Replacing "away."

The horses came as ordered, and his Lordship went with them that night unto Coll. Lanes at Bentley. And that same night, when John got back to Boscobell, he found the King there. When John had acquainted His Majestie with all which had passed, and where he had left my Lord Wilmot, His Majestie (supposing my Lord still at Moseley) dispatched John thither to him, with order to take som present course for his speedy remove, being forced back and set round on every side with dangers.

Mr. Whitgreeve and Mr. Hodleston, Saturday, that night after the parting with my Lord, went together to Mr. Hodlestons chamber, there reflecting upon the sad prospect [11] of affairs, the circumstance of the poor people about White-Ladies among whom the King was then left. And apprehending that happily they might be helpfull or serviceable som way or other, resolved [12] then, that in the morning by daylight they would goe thither. And in order therunto, met in the garden before sunrise. After a turn or two there, they observed one a good distance off, upon the footway which leads from White-ladies to the backside of Mr. Whitgreev's orchard. They, going thither out of the garden, discovered [13] the party to be John Pendrell. Who, observing Mr. Whitgreeve and Mr. Hodleston together, themselves [14] alone, approched and inquired after my Lord. They telling him his Lordship removed from us the night before, the [15] poor man, much struck and dejected therewith said: [16] "Then are wee all undon, for His Majestie is now forced back again to White-Ladies, weary, wett, enduring there hunger and cold all day long in the woods, no place to harbour him at night but som poor cotage or other, with dangers worse [17] then all other hardships: who hath sent me to my Lord to procure his speedy remove, not resolving which way to remove, nor wee able to advise."

Then Mr. Hodleston took him to his chamber, bid him rest there till wee had performd our duties to God for his

[11] Replacing "junctures."
[12] Replacing "resolved then that next morning by day was well was well light next morning to go thither and in order thereto."
[13] Replacing "to."
[14] Replacing "above."
[15] Replacing "wherat."
[16] Replacing "he."
[17] Replacing "which."

Majesties preservation and safety, bid [18] him rest himself well: his obedience in [19] this would bee more [20] acceptable to God then [21] his prayers, though Sunday, for he had laboured all that night and the day before and rest was most necessary, and [22] wee would pray for him.

Mr. Whitgreve and Mr. Hodleston having don their devotions (John well rested and refreshed, the people returnd from the church and in their houses at dinner), went with him to Bentley, where [23] my Lord resolved that Mr. Whitgreve should attend his Lordship about [24] 12 of the clock that night at his usuall stand, and that Richard and John Pendrell should bring his Majestie to such a stand as Mr. Hodleston should show John to bring him unto. Which was all observed. My Lord and Mr. Whitgreve were punctuall at their time and place, and his Majestie, about 3 of the clock in the morning, was receaved by Mr. Whitgreve and Mr. Hodleston at his stand [25] and by them conducted to my Lord. Mr. Whitgreve steept a litle before to give his Lordship notice that his friend was coming upstairs. The King was in my Lord's chamber, had his arm over my Lord's shoulder, and kissed him upon his cheek before my Lord was well aware, my Lord's back being towards the door when the King stept in.

There my Lord declared unto them that [26] the person there under that disguise was his maister and theirs, and the maister of us all. They kneeling down, his Majesty honoured them with his hand to kiss, bid them arise, told them hee had receaved so signall remarks of their loyalty [27] and affection to him, that hee should never be unmindfull therof. Then desired to see the Secret wherwith my Lord had acquainted him, that hee might be more ready to retreat when occasion required. Wherwith his Majestie seemed well pleased: and though a most sory place for the

---

[18] Replacing "it being Sunday."
[19] Replacing "then."
[20] Replacing "as."
[21] Replacing "as."
[22] Replacing "for."
[23] Replacing "his."
[24] Replacing "that night."
[25] Replacing "place."
[26] Replacing "who."
[27] Replacing "affection."

majestie of a King, yet upon occasions was well contented to retire.

After which, His Majestie returnd to his chamber, sate down upon the side of the bed, eate som biscot, and drunk a glass of sack; and bled a litle at his nose, brought out a handkerchiff, à la mode to his other attyre, upon which Mr. Hodleston receaved the blood, presented him with a faire one, and keept the other to himself. His Majestie bid him not concern himself, that was usuall to him. Then went to the fier, sat down in a chair there prepared, gave Mr. Hodleston leave to take off his shoes and stockings: his shoes were cutt and slasht, as well over his toes as behinde in the heels, to give ease to his feet, grown [28] tender with his uneasy night's marches on foot; much gravell got into his shoes, which were as wet within as without. The stockings he had then on were a paire of white flannen stockings next his skin, which his Majestie said he used with his boots with great embroidered topps; which they were glad to cutt off, having no other ready to use. Over them were a pair of old sad [29] gray stir-upd stockings, much dearnd in the knees, the heels and forefeet cut off; which in his march toward Wales, he was advised to draw over his own, to obscure the whitenes of [30] his own, which gave too great a show. On the night when Mr. Hodleston came to turn [31] off his Majesties own stockings, he [32] found litle roules of paper between them and his feet; [33] and marveling therat,[34] His Majestie told them he was advised to put white paper between as remedy,[35] the [36] most excellent remedy for the chafing of his feet.

Mr. Hodleston, having put a quission [37] and pillow under his feet, dryed them well with warm cloths, warmd [38] a paire of clean linnen stockings of Mr. Whitgrevs, a pare of large woosted

[28] Replacing "som ease."
[29] Replacing "stirrupt" ("sad" means "dark").
[30] Replacing "them which them."
[31] Replacing "turnd."
[32] Replacing "which were next to his skin."
[33] Replacing "toes."
[34] Replacing "with which they."
[35] Replacing "an excellent."
[36] Replacing "for the chafing of his feet."
[37] I.e., cushion.
[38] Replacing "put him on."

stockings of his own, and upon them a paire of new slippers of Mr. Whitgrevs. His Majestie, wherein finding himself at more ease, rose up and said he was then fit for a new march.

Mr. Hodleston also observing that the coursnes of his shirt did discompose him more then a little and hindered his rest, asked my Lord if that might not be changed. My Lord said, "Yes, by all means," and that he should be glad to change his own also, for since he came out of Scotland he had not shifted himself. Then Mr. Hodleston (having receaved half a dozen of new shirts only three daies before) brought [39] two of them, aired one well for his Majestie, which his Majestie was pleased to give [40] Mr. Hodleston leave to put upon himself. Which don, he aired the other and presented that to my Lord.

Munday morning. The day begining to appear, the Pendrells were dismissed, a bed in the Secret prepared by Mr. Whitgreeve and Mr. Hodleston; where his Majestie, after a short report and before any were stiring in the house, was pleased to retyre, as most quiet from any disturbance [41] to himself or the house, and securest from all other surprizes.

Mr. Hodleston having then Sir John Preston under his chardge, Tho. Paling and Frank Reynolds, two nephews of Mr. Whitgreeve, his companions, about 8 or 9 of the clock that morning, instead of learning their lessons, set those three boyes centry at three garret-windows which had full vew of the avenues to the house, ordered them to give him timely warning [42] of any that came near, and [43] what sort of persons they were. In which duty, the best soldiers of all could not be more diligant or exact then those three ladds for those two daies, wherein his Majestie was necessitated somtimes to withdraw, yet never with any either surprize to himself or disturbance at all to the house, Mr. Hodleston having alwais warning sufficient by one or other of the boyes before there was any need to withdraw.

Soldiers this day came about the house, took Mr. Whitgreeve away, urged he was a papist had been an officer in the

[39] Replacing "fetched."
[40] Replacing "put."
[41] Replacing "any all."
[42] Replacing "notice."
[43] Replacing "the he."

Kings army and at Worcester fight; but satisfyed by his neighbours that he was an infirm peaceable man and had not at all stirred from home, they dismissed him.[44] Which proved (as it happened) for the best, for by this means he got the freedom to stir abrode, not only to hear how all passed but likewise to send in provision, which then was to be done with all caution.

Mistris Whitgreeve during the time kept constantly with hir servants below stairs, ordering them and preparing what her son sent in for his guests, Mr. Hodleston constantly attending his Majestie above; not any other in that house, save only them three, ever privie to his Majesties presence[45] there, ever seeing his Majestie or having the least suspicion of his beeing in that house; but believing, as they heard from Mistris Whitgreeve and her son, that the strangers above with[46] Mr. Hodleston were Sir Wm. Hodleston and his son, who had been all along with King[47] Charls the First in his warrs, had engaged in this expedition with his son, and upon this defeat were retired[48] unto him till the countrey were a litle more at quiet.

This day likewise, John Pendrell was commanded to Coll. Lane's, with order to send my Lord's horses that night to the place appointed, where Mr. Whitgreeve would attend them. Upon that,[49] Lord Wilmot goes to Bentley with orders to send the Collonel next night to conduct his Majestie from Mr. Whitgrevs to Bentley.

Tuesday, September 9. His[50] Majestie spent most part of this day in Mr. Hodleston's chamber, reposing upon his bed and diverting himself with him in the window of a closet in the next room, just over the porch of the door which enters the hall, where his Majestie had a view of the equipage wherin severall of his poor soldiers marched off from Worcester, all of them stript, many of them cutt, som without stocking or shoe, scarce[51] so much left

---

[44] Other accounts report this as occurring the next day.
[45] Replacing "being."
[46] Replacing "were freends or relations."
[47] Replacing "the Kings father."
[48] Replacing "fled."
[49] Manuscript "them."
[50] Replacing "This day His Majestie spent most part of this day in Mr. Hodlestons chamber, Reposing Himself sometimes upon the ⟨his⟩ Bed and somtimes diverting himself with him."
[51] Replacing "or."

upon them as to cover their nakednes, eating pease out of reaps and handfulls of straw in their hands, which they had pulld up in the fields as they passed, roots and raw coleworts cast out of gardens for hoggs, and gathered up by them in the waies as they passed, to preserve themselves from famin, not dareing to call at any house, scarce to beg bread or touch anything but what was given them by good people of pitie. Som of them His Majestie knew, pointed at, and said they were Highlanders of his own regiment, and one of them an officer.

These [52] two daies, Mr. Hodleston pretended indisposition, not only to bring Mistris Whitgreeve and her son to keep him company at mealetimes in his chamber, where His Majestie constantly eate during the time of his stay, but likewise to prevent the coming up of any servant. [53]

Mistris Whitgreve, in the kitching, acted in chief, dressed [54] and dished all herself. Her son handed it [55] all upstairs, and Mr. Hodleston from his chamber door to the table. His Majestie ordered Mistris Whitgreve to com up; commanded her to sit downe at table and [56] to carve for his Majestie and my Lord, which she did with a very good heart.

About twelve of the clock that night, the Collonel came to the place wher Mr. Whitgreve was [57] waiting: who took the Collonel to the corner of his orchard, where the Collonel would stay till Mr. Whitgreeve had acquainted his Majestie with the Collonel's being there.

---

[52] This paragraph and the following one replace this much-amended version: "These two daies Mr. Hodleston pretended indisposition, not only to draw Mistris Whitgreve and her son to keep him company at ~~table~~ meale times in his chamber, where His Majestie did constantly eate during ~~his stay~~ the time of his stay ⟨but likewise⟩ and to prevent the coming up of any servant, Mistris Whitgreeve herself ~~below herself did~~ dishd up all ~~below~~ in the kitching ⟨below⟩, ~~herself,~~ her son handed it ⟨from⟩ thence, ~~and~~ upstairs, and Mr. Hodleston from his chamber door to the table. His Majestie ⟨ordered⟩ ~~commanded~~ Mistres Whit. to com up, ~~both~~ commanded her to set ~~downe~~ with him at table and carve for himself and my Lord, which she did with a very good heart.

[53] "Or other" is struck out after "servant."

[54] Replacing "directed."

[55] Replacing "from thence all."

[56] Replacing "the table with his Majestie and to carve for his Majestie."

[57] Replacing "attended."

Then [58] his Majestie, having [59] thanked Mistris Whitgreeve, her son, and Mr. Hodleston for their fidelity, care, and pains, took leave of Mistris Whitgreeve. Mr. Hodleston and her son, attending his Majestie to the Collonel in the orchard, told the Collonel who the person was they there presented unto him: so the Collonel and they attended his Majestie to his horse.

Mr. Hodleston, considering the coldnes of the misselling moist night, the unusuall thinnes of his Majesties attyre, took along [60] with him his cloke upon [61] his arm; and when his Majestie was ready to take horse, presented him with it, which his Majestie took about him.

So having made their obeysance there againe to his Majestie, praying for his Majesties prosperous journey and safety, his Majestie, mounting his horse, took leave of them and rode away with Coll. Lane: who afterwards return'd the cloke to Mr. Whitgreve by John Pendrell.

And if it would please God ever to bless him but with ten or twelve thousand men of a minde and resolved to fight, he should not doubt but to drive these rogues out of the land. [62]

Notes from Father Hurlston [63]

The king is mistaken in calling Mr. Whitgr[ave] Mr. Pitchcross.

The like in calling his mother for grand-mo[ther].

There was onely one brother, viz. Sir Jo. Preston, under his care, then about 10 years old; and the other were Francis Raynolds and Thomas Payly, two nephews of Mr. Whitgrave, play-fello[ws] to Sir J. P.

Raynolds was very serviceable in hold[ing] the King's horses

[58] Replacing "Hereupon."
[59] Replacing "thereupon."
[60] Replacing "his own cloke."
[61] Replacing "under his."
[62] This paragraph is added in the margin of the entry relating to Sunday, but since it does not fit in with the matter there, it is here put at the end of Father Huddleston's report.
[63] The sheets on which these notes are written are broken at the edges, so that many words are deficient. The present edition gives, in square brackets, what are likely to have been the original readings.

and watching, and has received considera[ble] kindness from the King since, by an office which [he] has since lost as being a Catholick.

That all the persons employd in this wo[rk], within the knowledge of Father H., were Rom[an] Catholicks but Mr. Huntbatch.

Father H. his name is John Hodlestone [and h]is branch of the family, which is distinguished [by the] name of Hutton-John, the name of a mann[or in] Cumberland. His grandfather was halfe-brother, by a second venture, to Sir Wm. Hurlston, who with eight brothers raised two regiments for the King and served with them. And himselfe came in with Sir Jo. Preston under the [Duke] of Newcastle, and continued actually in the war till after Hambleton-war, which was the [last] that the King had, when Hambleton was [lost] and the old King taken. He came in in the beginning of the war.

The habit that the King came in to [Fath]er H. was a very greasy old gray steeple [tu]rned hat, with the brims turned up, without [lini]ng or hat-band, the swett appearing two inches [deep] ⟨through it⟩ round the band-place; a green cloth jump-coat, thread-bare, even to the threads being worne whi[te]; and breeches of the same, with [64] long knees downe to the [gar]ter; with an old swetty leather doublet, a pair of white flannell-stockings next his leggs, which the King said were his boote-stockings, their tops being cutt off to pre-vent their being discover'd; and upon them, a paire of old green yarne stockings, all worne, and dearned at the knees, w[ith] their feet cutt off; which last he said he had of Mr. Woolf, who perswaded him thereto, to hi[de] his other white ones, for feare of being observed. His shoes were old, all slasht for the ease of h[is] feet and full of gravell, with little rowlls of pa[per] between his toes; which he said he was advised to, to keep them from galling. He had an old course shirt, patched both at the neck and hands, of th[at] very course sort which in that country go by the name of nogging-shirts. Which shirt Father H. shifting from the King (by giving him one of h[is] own new ones), Father H. sent afterwards to Mr. Sherw[ood, no]w Lord Abbot of Lambspring in Germany, a person well knowne to the Duke, who begg'd this shirt of Father H. His handkerchief was a very old one, torne and very course; and being [d]awbed with the King's blood from his nose, Father H. gave it to a kinswoman of his, one Mr. Brithwayte, who kept it with great [ven]eracion, as a remedy for the King's Evil. He had no gloves, but a long thorn-stick, not very strong, but crooked [th]ree or four severall ways, in his hand; his [ha]ir cutt short up to his ears, and hands coloured, his Majesty refusing to have any gloves

[64] Replacing "and."

when Fath[er H.] offered him some, as also to change his stick.

Father H. observes very particularly, as [an] extraordinary instance of God's providence in this [a]faire, the contingency of his first meeting w[ith] Jo. Penderell, occasioned [65] by one Mr. Garrett's comeing [66] the Thursday after the fight out of Warwickshire from Mrs. Morgan, grandmother to little Sir Jo. Preston, with some new linnen for Sir Jo. and some for Father H. himselfe, namely, six new shirts, one whereof he gave to the King and another to my Lord Wilmot.

This Sir Jo. Preston's father was Sir J. P., who raised a regiment for the King; and for so doing had his estate given away by the Parliament to Pin. This Sir J. P. son is since dead, and his estate falne to his brother, Sir Tho. P., mencioned in Oates's Narrative of the Plott, who married my Lord Molinux his daughter, by whom he had two daughters, great heiresses, himselfe being become Jesuite.[67]

S. P.[68] desireing to know from Father Hurlstone what he knew touching the brotherhood of the Penderells, as to [the] names and quallitys of each of the brothers; he answered that he was not very perfect in it, but that as far as he could recollect, they were thus, viz.

1st. William the eldest, who lived at Boscobell.
2.   John, who lived at White-Ladys, a kinde of woodward [69] there, all the brothers liveing in the wood, haveing little farmes there, and labouring for theire liveing in cutting downe of wood and watching the wood from being stolne, haveing the benefit of some cow-grass to live on. Father H. further told me that here lived one Mr. Walker, an old gentlemen, a preist, whither the poor Catholiques in that neighbour-hood ⟨resorted⟩ for devotion and [70] whome Father H. used now and then to visit and say prayers and doe holy offices with. Upon which score it was that John Pendrell happened to know him in the high-way when the said P. was lookeing out for a hideing place for my Lord Wilmot.

⟨This John was he, as Father H. says, that tooke the most pai[ns] of all the brothers.⟩

[65] Replacing "viz., that the Thursday after the Fight."
[66] Replacing "came."
[67] This paragraph and the preceding one are given as footnotes in Dalrymple's edition, but wrongly credited to Pepys himself.
[68] From this point to the end of Father Huddlestone's notes, the handwriting is Pepys's own. So too are the changes and additions—enclosed by angle brackets—in the notes up to this point.
[69] I.e., a woodkeeper.
[70] Replacing "[resorted] whether Father."

3. Richard, comonly called among them "tru[sty] Richard," who
    lived the same kinde of life with [the rest].

4. Humphrey, a miller, who has a son at this day a footman to the
    Queen, to be heard of at Sommersett-House.

5. George, another brother, who was in some degree ⟨less or more⟩,
    as he remembers, imployed in this service.

        He thinks there was a sixth brother, but of that is not
    certaine.[71]

        Q. Who was Collonel Carlos, and what part acted he in this
    matter?

    Ditto. Concerning one Yates,[72] that marryed a sister of one of
    the Penderells? to whom Father H says he has heard that
    the old course shirt [73] which the King had on did belong;
    and [con]sequently, that the King did shift himself at his
    ho[use]. But beleives that the rest of the King's cloathes were
    William Penderells, he being a tall man, and the breeches
    the King had on being very long at [the] Knees.

[71] Blount says he was Thomas, who fought for Charles I at
Edgehill and died there.
[72] This Francis Yates was married to Margaret (Penderel) and lived
at Langley Lawn, near White Ladies. It was another Francis Yates,
apparently, who joined with Charles Giffard in guiding the King from
Worcester to White Ladies.
[73] Replacing "Shift."

～VIII～
THOMAS WHITGREAVE,
An Account of Charles the Second's Preservation

Thomas Whitgreave's *Account* does not appear in Pepys's collection of documents related to the King's escape. However, Lady Tuke enquired whether Pepys thought it necessary for a copy of Huddlestone's report to be sent to Whitgreave, and the appearance of his name as giving personal testimony for *A Summary of Occurences* in 1688 implies that sometime after Lady Tuke's letter Whitgreave put his account into writing. The present editor knows no evidence to support Sir Arthur Bryant's flat statement that this was one of the authentic accounts that Pepys secured and placed on record, though it is known he was seeking it. The inclusion of the report here may be justified on the grounds that Pepys may have instigated it and expected Whitgreave to send it to him.

Whitgreave's own story was first printed as "A Simple and Circumstantial Narrative," communicated by one of his descendants to *The Gentleman's Magazine* in July 1789. This was reprinted in *The Retrospective Review*, XIV; J. Hughes, *The Boscobel Tracts* (London, 1830 and 1857); and Allan Fea's *After Worcester Fight* (London, 1904). The present text is taken from the first printing, which states that the original was in Thomas Whitgreave's handwriting, on six separate folio sheets, written on one side only and numbered one to six in the manner of counsellor's briefs: the endorsement reads, "An Account of King Charles the Second Preservacion."

The narrative relates to the first week of the King's escape and mainly to his stay at Moseley Hall.

K ing Charles the Second comeing from Worcester fight, being Wednesday, Sept. 3, 1651, about sun-rising next morning, being Thursday, by the conduct of Mr. Charles Giffard, and his man Yates, arrived at White Ladyes, where, as soon as might bee, he was divested of his apparell, his hayr cut of, and habited like a country fellow; which being done, haveing taken leave of the lords who attended him, was committed to the charge of the Pendrells. The Lords, &c. then most of them fled after the flying armye towards Newport, and so Northwards. The Lord Willmott was re-

Thursday   solved to fly counter towards London, and so by the guidance of John Pendrell gott to Mr. Hunt-baches of Brinsford; from whence he sent the said Pendrell to Wolverhampton and all his acquaintance thereabouts, to gett some Azilum for him; but not prevayling, as he was returning back, hee met with Mr. Hudelston (whom hee had seen formerly att White Ladyes), with young Sir John Preston, to whose custody hee was committed by Mrs. Morgan, of Weston, grand mother to him, and sent to my mother's to table, for fear Pym should seize him going there, by the name of Jackson; for whose companions Mr. Huddleston was pleased to admit Mr. Francis Raynolds and Mr. Tho. Palin, both nephews of mine, and to teach them with him, and asked him what news hee heard, who answered none but very good; which was, the King had gott the day at Worcester. But Pendrell answered, 'tis clean contrarie; and then related to him the said news of his Majesties defeat att Worcester the day before; and how, that morning earlie, the King came to White Ladyes, and was with some of his brothers in disguise, and that my Lord of Cleveland; but indeed, Willmott hee left att the said Huntbaches, and was by him sent to Hampton,[1] and to all his acquaintance thereabout, to gett some secrett place to secure him: which not being able to do, he asked Mr. Huddles-

[1] I.e., Wolverhampton.

ton whether his landlord, being myself, would do him the favour to secure him; who replyed, I will take you to him, and you shall see. Upon their arrivall, Mr. Huddleston told me all the sad news, and his buisines with me; whereupon I said I would with speed wait on his Lordship; which I did accordingly: and when there, Mr Huntbach brought mee to his chamber, whom, after I had condoled his Majesties and all his friends sad misfortunes, I told him I feared not to secure his Lordship if I could gett privately to my house, which I thought the best way was for mee to wish Mr Huntbach to bring him a by way to a close of mine, called The Moore, about midnight, where att thatt tyme I would wait for him, and take him to a friend's house not far of, wheare I feard not his securitie (to conceal from Mr. Huntbach my taking him home), where accordingly I wayted for their comeing 2 or 3

Thursday howers; and then, supposing they had steared some other course, I returned home, where I found my Lord Willmott arrived, being conducted by the said Huntbach an other way along the publick ways and lanes, which when my Lord understood, he was much troubled.

Friday The next morning, I sent a messenger[2] well known to Col. Lane, to acquaint him that my Lord was with mee, but I had no conveniency for his horses, my howse lying to the open roade, and an howse over against itt, and therefore I desired him to entertain them (they being that night att one Evans house, a poor man nigh Mr. Huntbach), myself being better able to secure my lord than them, who seemed very willing, and bidd the messenger bring them, and that att night he would himself wait on his Lordship, and that I should, about midnight expect his comeing into a close called Allport's Leasow, wherein was a great drie pitt, covered with many trees, where the colonel accordingly came; and having tied his horse in the said pitt, I brought him through my back side to my Lord's chamber, who,

Friday night when they saw each other, they renewed their former acquaintance, the Colonel formerly having served in my Lord's brigade. The Colonel then invited my Lord to his house, as far more safe, my self, as hee stiled mee, a Papist, and more liable to searches; besides, his sister, the Lady Jane, had newlie gott a pass from Capt. Stone.

[2] Blount says this was William Walker.

governor of Stafford, for her self and a man to goe into the West, which might bee a convenient opportunity for his passage away. But the day before, I haveing shewn his Lordship a privacie in my house, formerly made in tymes of persecution, and in which, after the late unfortunate warre, I secured my self against the violent strict search of Capt. Stone's troop, his lordship so approved of itt for his securitie, that hee wished hee had given 100,000 friends of his were with him; gave the Colonel many thanks for his kind offer, but for the present said hee was well pleased and satisfied with his present quarters, but desired him to keep the opportunity of his sister's pass, and his horses, till hee heard from him again, and so took leave of him, and I conducted [him] back to his horses. This morning, being Friday, Jo. Pendrell came to my Lord, and staid all day with him, who att night sent him to White Ladyes, to enquire what was become of the king; who returned, and said he went from thence the night before to Madeley in Shropshire, with a design to gett over Severn, and so to steere for Wales (but Severn was so guarded he could not pass, but was forct to stay there all that night and next day [3] in a barn of Mr. Woolfs); of whose removeall as soon as my Lord heard, hee resolved speedily to remove to Col. Lane's, and wisht me to send to him to have his horses sent for him that night, which I did, and they came accordingly: and so, after many thanks for all my care and kind entertainment, haveing dismissed Jo. Pendrell, hee went, and safely arrived at the Colonel's the next morning. Mr. Huddleston and my self were walking in
Saturday   the long walk, and concluding in the afternoon
to go to White Ladyes, to receave a perfect relation of all the transactions there, where unexpectedly wee saw Jo. Pendrell comeing to us, and asking us where my
Sunday   Lord was, wee telling him he was gone from hence, he replyed, wee then are all undone, for att my return yesterday, there being no passage over Severn, the king was forct, on Friday night, to come back to Boscobell,[4] and there meet with Col. Carelos, and that they had no entertainment for him, neither knew they how to dispose of him, who grew very mellancholly upon itt: but hearing by mee that I left my lord here, hee

[3] Saturday night and Sunday: in fact, it was Thursday and Friday.
[4] He arrived on Saturday morning.

sent mee to his Lordship, to gett a place for his security with him here. Whereupon Mr. Huddleston and myself went with Pendrell to the Colonel, hee being a stranger to him, and we durst not write by him; where I being arrived, acquainted the

Sunday Colonel that Pendrell came to us from some person of eminent qualitie, whose name he was not to discover, to bring him to my Lord; and therefore I came with him my self, that hee should not be afraid to give admittance; whereupon, the colonel immediatlie took him to my Lord; who, after some private conference and direccions for Mr. Huddleston and myself, hee sent him to us, to return with speed, and in the way homewards to acquaint us the person hee came from was the king, which his Lordship till then never discovered; and that hee desired myself to attend his comeing that night, about an eleaven of clock, att his usual pitt in Alport's Leasow; and that Mr. Huddleston and self should appoint a place in my ground, whither hee and his brothers should bring the King, about 12 or one of clock that night: which wee accordingly did, and Pendrell speedily sent away to acquaint his Majestie. Att night, Mr. Huddleston and self, as soon as all the familie was gone to bedd, went to our severall stands, hee to a close called The Moor, and my self to the usual drie pitt. My Lord came punctually according to his howre, whom I brought up to his chamber, and after [5] the time prefixed, hee wisht mee to go to Mr. Huddleston, to see if they were come with his friend, as hee called him; but I returning, and telling him they were not, hee seemed much troubled, and apprehensive of his miscarriage; then, after a little while, hee wished mee to go again, and to stay in the orchard expecting [6] them, where, after a while, I saw them comeing up the long walke, which I speedily acquainted his Lordship with, who wished mee to stay att the orchard door, and to shew him the way to the stayrs, where my Lord expected him with a light. When hee came to the door, with the Pendrells guarding him, he was so habitted, like one of them, that I could not tell which was hee, only I knew all the rest, I could scarce putt off my hatt to him, but hee discovering by the light the stayrs, ymediatlie went to them, where his Lordship expected him, and took him up to his chamber: then I took the

[5] I.e., according to.
[6] I.e., awaiting.

Pendrells into the buttry, to eate and drink, that I might dispatch them away, and secure the house; but ere they had done, my Lord sent Mr. Huddleston down to mee, desireing mee to come up, which accordingly I did, and coming att the chamber door, his Majestie and my Lord being both att a cupboard's head nigh to itt, talking, his Lordship said to mee, this gentleman under disguize, whom I have hitherto concealed, is both your maister, mine, and the maister of us all, to whom wee all owe our duty and allegiance; and so, kneeling down, he gave me his hand to kiss, and bidd me arise, and said hee had receaved from my Lord such a character of my loyaltie and readines in those dangers to assist him and his friends, that hee would never been unmindful of mee or mine; and the next word after was, where is the private place my Lord tells me of? which being already prepared and shewed him, hee went into itt, and when come forth, said itt was the best place hee was ever in. Then hee returning to his chamber, sitting down by the fier side, wee pulled of his shoes and stockings, and washed his feet, which were most sadly galled, and then pulled of likewaies his apparell and shirt, which was of hurden cloth, and put him one of Mr. Huddleston's, and other apparell of ours; then, after he had refreshed himself a little, by eating some biskett, and drinking a glass of wine, hee grew very chearfull, and said, if itt would please Almighty God to send him once more an army of 10,000 good and loyall soldiers and subjects, he feared not to expell all those rogues forth of his kingdom: then, after an howres discourse or more, he was desirous to repose himself on a bedd that

Sunday night

night. The next day, the servants were sent all forth to work, onely the cook maid, a Catholike, kept within to gett provision, as pretended, for a relation of Mr. Huddleston's, who fled to him from Worcester fight: neither shee nor Mr. Huddleston's schollars admitted to his sight, nor having the least suspect [7] who hee was, the boys having, during his stay, liberty to play, and to watch who were comeing: whereupon Sir Jo. Preston one night att supper with the other boys said, eate hard, boys, for wee have been on the life guard and hard dutie this day (more trulie spoke then hee was aware). In the morning, my Lord took my mother to his

[7] I.e., suspicion.

Majestie, and acquainted him who shee was, who,
Monday   kneeling down to kiss hand, hee most gratiously
saluted, and when she had brought up dinner,
would have had her sitt down with him, Mr. Huddleston and myself wayting. In the afternoon I was sent to Hampton, to enquire
after news, and att my return wisht by my Lord to send for his
horses that night from Col. Lane's; which I did accordingly, and
he returned with them. All that night his Majestie lay
Night   on his bed, Mr. Huddleston watching within, and
myself without doors. The next morning, my studie-
door being open, his Majestie was pleased, with Mr. Huddleston
and self, to go into itt, and for diversion to look forth of it into
the court and com'on roade; where he saw many of his soldiers,
and some of his own regiment, which he knew, come up to the
doors, some for provisions and others for plaisters for their wounds.
There he told us of the Scotts usage, and of his march from thence
to Worcester, and of the fight there, and inquired of us how this
country and the gentry stood affected, and who were against him:
then looking upon severall books, hee saw Mr. Turbevill's Catech-
isme [8] and read a little of itt, said itt was a pretty book, and that
hee would take itt with him. In the afternoon, reposing himself
on his bed in the parlour chamber, and inclineing
Afternoon   to sleep, as I was watching at the window, one of
the neighbours I saw come running in, who told
the maid, soldiers were comeing to search, who thereupon presentlie came running to the staires head, and cried, soldiers, soldiers
are comeing; which his Majestie hearing, presentlie started out of
his bedd, and runn to his privacie, where I secured him the best
I could, and then leaving him, went forth into the street to meet
the soldiers, who were comeing to search, whom, as soon as they
saw, and knew who I was, were readie to pull mee in peeces, and
take mee away with them, saying I was come from the Worcester
fight; but after much dispute with them, and by the neighbours
being informed of their false information, that I was not there,
being very ill a great while, they lett me goe; but till I saw them
clearly all gone forth of the town, I returned not; but as soon as
they were, I returned to release him, and did acquaint him with

[8] Henry Turbeville, *Manual of Controversies.*

my stay, which hee thought long, and then hee began to bee very chearfull again. In the interim, whilst I was disputing with soldiers, one of them, called Southall, came in the fould, and asked a smith, as hee was shooing horses there, if he could tell where the king was, and hee should have a thowsand pounds for his payns, as the smith, called Holbeard, since severall times hath told mee and others. This Sowthall was the great priest-catcher, and Capt. Lane's and Mr. Vernon's true cavaleer in the plotting time. That afternoon my lord sent word he would send Col. Lane

Thursday night

with an horse for the King about midnight, and that I must expect him att the usual place. At night his Majestie wisht Mr. Huddleston to shew him our oratory, saying, hee knew hee was a priest, and hee needed not to fear to own itt to him, for if it pleased God to restore him to his kingdom, wee should never need more privacies; who having seen it, said itt was a very decent place. Afterwards I went to the Colonel, and took a nephew, Mr. Fra. Raynolds, with mee, to hold the horses whilst the Colonel went up to the house with mee; who arriving, I brought him to the orchard stile, where he would stay and expect till we brought his Majestie to him; of which I acquainting his Majestie, he sent mee for my mother to come to take leave of him, who bringing with her some raysings, almonds, and other sweetmeats, which shee presenting to him, some whereof hee was pleased to eat, and some took with him; afterwards, wee all kneeling down and praying Almighty God to bless, prosper, and preserve him, hee was pleased to salute my mother, and give her thanks for his kind entertainment; and then giving his hand to Mr. Huddleston and my self to kiss, saying, if itt pleased God to restore him, hee would never be unmindfull of us, hee took leave and went, conducted with Mr. Huddleston and self, to the colonel, and thence to his horses expecting him, where hee having gott on horseback, wee kneeled, and kiss his hand again, offering all our prayers for his safetie and preservacion, Mr. Huddleston putting on him a cloak of his, to keep him from cold and wett, which afterwards, by the Colonel's order, was sent to mee, wee took leave.

~IX~

THE ALFORD DEPOSITIONS

This group of documents consists of a paper from Captain Gregory Alford and two letters written by Joseph Taylor and his father. All of them were given to Pepys by Alford, and Pepys appends a memorandum giving further details on the matter in concern.

The documents all refer to incidents during the King's stay at Trent, particularly to the abortive attempt to escape by boat from Charmouth with the assistance of William Ellesdon and Stephen Limbry. The explanation of that failure which appears in these documents is so unflattering to Ellesden and so radically different from the picturesque reason that Ellesden himself gives, that it has been thought only decent to give in an appendix to this group the relevant part of Ellesdon's explanation. This is taken from Alexander M. Broadley, *The Royal Miracle* (London, 1912).

The documents in Pepys's collection are in a clerk's hand, with a few minor additions in another hand. They were printed in Henry Cary's *Memorials of the Great Civil War in England* (London, 1842), from a Tanner manuscript in the Bodleian Library which was copied early in the eighteenth century from the Pepys copies.

The documents were delivered to Pepys on December 22, 1684. They are the latest of his collection, and it may be assumed that he then thought that they completed his work on the King's escape and that he ordered the collection to be bound early the next year.

A Paper from Captain Alford, praesent Mayor of Lyme, 1684, relateing to some perticulars in the King's escape from Worcester.

The Right Honourable the Lord Keeper of the Great Seale of England, having desired mee to give him an accompt of what I know of his Majesty's most miraculous escape, and the great dangers he passed through after he came from Worcester, I doe here doe it, viz.

His Majesty came to that loyal gentleman's house, Sir Frances Windham, at Trent in the County of Sommersett within three Miles from Sheerborne; and being there, his Majesty, well knowing the great trust he might repose in Collonel Gyles Strangwayes, sent Sir Frances Windham to consult with him as to his preservation and escape, and to send him what money he could. The sayd Collonel's father being then living, he had no great command of money, and for reasons then best known to himselfe could not comunicate such a secrett to his father; but readily fetched £100 in gold, protesting it was all hee had, and delivered it to Sir Frances Windham. And they then consulting the most safest way for his Majesty's imbarquacion, they thought that about Lime there might be some convenient place, if they could finde a fitt man that might be trusted.

Then the Collonel advised[1] that one Captain Alford, whome his Majesty well knew to be a fitt person to be intrusted; or if hee were not to be found, then he knew of noe other but Mr. Wm. Elesdon, that lived in Lyme. Soe one Peters, a servant to Sir Frances Windham, was sent to find out Captain Alford; who was then in Portugall, forced to be abroad by reason of his loyalty; but Elesdon being newly married to a very rich but riged presbiterian. Soe Sir Francis Windham came and conferred with Mr. Elesdon

---

[1] The King and Anne Wyndham say that Strangways made no suggestions at all.

for the transporting, as hee sayd, beyond the sea of two gentlemen, and desired him to freight some barke for that purpose.

Mr. Elesdon addressd himself to one Stephen Limbry, who was master of a small barke of 30 tunn to whom he declared that there were two gentlemen that desired passage into any part of France: the one, having marryed a great fortune, was troubled by her father and friends, and soe they would goe into France for some time. They treated on the conditions; which were, that whereas Limbry was then bound for St. Mallo, he should putt out those goods which he had on board, and should ballast his shipp at Mr. Elesdon's cost, who promised to give the sayd master £25 in hand and an obligacion to pay him £25 more when hee should bring him a note or letter that hee had safely landed them in any port of France.[2]

This agreement being made, the master fitted out his shipp. Of which notice was given to Sir Frances Windham, who with his Majesty came to a small house belonging to Mr. Elesdon's brother (who was a then violent Oliverian) about two miles from Lyme, where he gave an account of what was done as to the freighting the ship. Soe Elesdon went for Lyme and told the master that the gentlemen were come, and that they would be at Charmouth at 5 of the clock that night, and that he should not faile to be there at that time to meet him, and he would there pay him the £25 and give him his security for the other £25. But the master demanding his charges in ballasting his shipp, which was but 9s, Mr. Elesdon refused to pay it; for which the master was discontented.

Yett the master (whose dwelling was at Charmouth) failed not to be there, and came severall times to the house where the gentlemen were with the lady, Mrs. Coningsby (who is now Mr. Hixe's wife), and demanded of the people of the house if Mr. Elesdon were come. The King spoake with the master, who assured him his ship was ready; but still hee lingred to see when Mr. Elesdon would come to fulfill his agreement. And it being very late at night, the master finding that Mr. Elesdon never came, who had not payd (nor never did any other) one penny of the money, the

<hr/>

[2] Ellesden gives no financial details, apart from "an ample reward." Anne Wyndham says £60 was to be paid by Ellesdon on Limbry's return.

master retired to his house after he had been there three times, and never came againe to the King.

So his Majesty, finding himself to be deluded, was now to consult his further preservacion. Command was given that theyr horses should be made ready. But it was found that the Kings horse, which carryed double, had a shooe loose. Soe a smith was sent for, who comeing and lookeing over the shooes of all the horses, sayd he knew that all those horses had been shod about Worcester. Yett he fastned the shooes, and presently went to consult with one Westly the parson of Charmouth (a ridged foolish Presbiterian), who was then in a long-winded prayer. And before he had done, the King was gone towards Bridport, intelligence being carryed into Lime, which is a mile and halfe from Charmouth, but by what meanes it's not knowne—on which ten or twelve troopers were despatched away to pursue them.[3]

The King stopped at Bridport at the George Inne. My Lord Wilmott and Sir Francis Windham went up into a roome with the lady, as masters. To the groome (who was the King) they left to see the horses well rubbed. They commanded a sholder of mutton to be made ready. The oastler took very great notice of the pretended groome, and told him hee was formerly a soldier for the King in Exon, and cursed the Parliaments soldiers that were then in the house, still urgeing on the King that hee had seen him in Exon.[4] Insomuch, that the King was forced to call to mind where he lodged in Exon, and told him that he had lived in Exon with one Mr. George Potter, and had been his groome. The oastler replyed that he knew well Mr. Potter and Captain Alford that marryed Mrs. Potters daughter. Soe on this acquaintance, the canns were called for and they drank lovingly together.

In a short time, the mutton being ready, the King was called up, who made hast to eat (the door being shutt), and soe

[3] Ellesdon and Anne Wyndham say the smith was Hammet (Hamnet) of Charmouth and the horse was Wilmot's. Anne Wyndham says the troopers were led by Captain Macy, to whom the ostler told his suspicions; but Ellesdon says the captain was roused to action by Hamnet and Parson Westly.

[4] I.e., Exeter. This incident, although related by the King, is lacking in Ellesdon's and Anne Wyndham's narratives.

went againe to fitt the horse. Whilest they did eate, they took care (the house being full of soldiers) to be served by an old woman, to whome they gave the rest of the mutton, who took out the pann of the close-stoole to hide it away under.

They made haste to take horse, and rid away on London road a little way. But at the first turning on the left hand, they left that road and went bye-wayes to Broad-Windsor, which was clear back againe, and in the evening came to the George Inne there, which was well knowne to Sir Francis Windham. But it hapned that the house was full of troopers, so that there was but a little topp-chamber that could be had for the King and his company, and but one bedd. It fell out that night that a woman in the house fell in travail, soe that the troopers were gone to other houses. Soe his Majesty took horse in the morning, with the gentlewoman behind him, and arrived safe at Sir Francis Wind- ham's at Trent. [5]

His Majesty had not been gon out of Bridport a quarter of an hour, before 12 troopers of Lyme were come to pursue after those gentlemen that had laine at Charmouth. They made enquiry at the inne, and were there informed that the said gentlemen were gone downe the towne on London road. Soe they made great speed after them, and never stop't till they came to Dorchester, not thinking they had made such a turning back. Mr. Elesdon, finding that the King was gone, and that the Lyme troopers were returned, tooke horse himselfe. And being half a mile from the towne of Lyme, mett with one Mr. Tho. Taylor, whome he desired to goe with him, telling him that there was £1000 to be gott for whoever should take the King, and he knew where he was. But the sayd Mr. Taylor refused to goe with him, saying he would not do it if it were to gaine the world.

So Mr. Elesdon went forward and came to Sir Hugh Windham's house at Bilsdon,[6] five miles from Lyme and two miles from Broad-Windsor, thinking the King had been there. He went in boldly, and asked of Sir Hugh Windham or his lady [7] for

---

[5] These incidents at Broad Windsor are also related by Ellesdon and Anne Wyndham, although not by the King.

[6] I.e., Pilisdon House.

[7] The phrase "or his lady" is added in Alford's own hand.

the King; who replyed to him that he was a base fellow, to come to his house to aske for the King, and soe commanded him out of his house.

The sayd Elesdon was gon [8] but a little time before the troopers (which had pursued the King before from Bridport) were come into the house of Sir Hugh Wyndham and made dilligent search.[9] They did not spare the young ladyes, as Sir Frances Windham hath sayd; and the gentleman, Mr. Hixt (that since marryed Mrs. Conningsby, both living), hath affirmed that he hath often heard his wife say what is above inserted of what past at Sir Hugh Windhams, for shee was told it after the King's escape by Sir Hugh and the ladyes that were soe used by the troopers.

Limbry the master, since his Majesty's happy Restauracion, hath deposed before a Master of Chancery, in the presence of severall persons now living, that directly or indirectly he never received one penny of money of Mr. Elesdon nor of any other on the sayd contract, but that he had carryed away the gentlemen soe-called had he had the money agreed on, which hee was to receive at Charmouth, and that whatever hath been sett forth to the contrary was notoriously false; and layd the blame wholly on Mr. Elesdon for not comeing to Charmouth to have performed the agreement made with him.

That Mr. Robert Ewell of Marshalsay, the 10th of April, 1684, sayd that he had been often told by Abraham Poger that Mr. Elsdon's tenant at Wilde came to him and told him that the King was at his house, and desired his advice whether hee should gett him taken. Poger told him, as hee was come for safety and his roof, he should in no wise betray him but lett him goe as hee came, and it would be the price of blood, and it would doe no good, perswaded him to desist. Benjamin Bird was with mee, comeing from Sherburne, when the words were spoken by Elwell.

That Stephen Limbray often told Captain Fookes that if Elsdon had payd him but £10,[10] he had carryed away the King;

[8] Replacing "not."
[9] Ellesdon himself says nothing about his going to Pilisdon, but Anne Wyndham reports the troopers' search and Ellesdon's visit.
[10] Replacing "what."

and so he told Mr. Tho. Plucknell, who spake it at Bridport the 22nd of January, 1683, before the Lord Bishop of Bristoll; and Mr. Jones [11] doth affirme that the master often told him that if Elesdon would have given him but £5, he had proceeded.

The above I doe affirm hath ben offten told me

Gregory Alford [12]

A COPY OFF JOSEPH TAYLORS LETTER
TO HIS FATHER[13]

The Captain presses me very much to write to you, to have me certify all the passages that were betweene Mr. Elesden and me, which the Captain sayes you have often told him was, vizt. In the yeare 1654, presently after the newes of his Majesty's happy escape from Worcester and of the newes of some gentlemen that had in a day or two before been at Charmouth (you having been out of Lyme, and were comeing home againe within half a mile from the towne) you mett with Mr. Wm. Elesdon, who came from the towne and would have perswaded you to goe along with him, for that there was a proclamacion read that whoever could take the King should have £1000 reward; but you refused to goe, saying you would not doe it if it were to gaine the World. So you parted. Now, Sir, if all these circumstances be not true, you may be pleased to certify what is the whole truth of it as soon as you please. Which is all at present from,

Your

[11] This may be Rice Jones, landlord of the inn at Broad Windsor.
[12] This affirmation and signature are in Alford's own hand.
[13] This heading is added in Alford's hand.

MY LORD KEEPER[14] HATH THIS LETTER UNDER MR. TAYLOR'S HAND.

I do here declare, as I doe minde the words long since when I mett with Mr. Wm. Elesden rideing, one was rideing forth and the other into the towne of Lyme, Mr. Elesdon his words, unexpected of mee, "Now, Mr. Taylor, there is a £1000 promised for anyone that can discover the King," my answer to him: "I would not do it if it were to gaine the World," and so parted. I referr myselfe to the words I gave under my hand to the captain long since, when the words were fresher in my memory then now.

The first part is what Joseph writt his father from London, the second is what Mr. Tayler says in answer,

This paper I gave in.
Gregory Alford.[15]

YORKE-BUILDINGS, DECEMBER 22TH 1684

Memorandum. That this day Captain Alford did signe the foregoing papers and delivered them me soe signed, telling mee that hee had come to the knowledge of the contents of the sayd papers by his frequent discourse since concerning this matter with Sir Francis Windham and Collonel Strangwayes, and more perticularly from his being called to a hearing had before the Lord Chancellor in the plague yeare, 1665, when the Court was at Oxford by command of the King, upon occasion of some misunderstandings between the sayd Sir Francis Windham and Collonel Strangways, the former

[14] "Keeper" added by Alford.
[15] The attestation and signature are in Alford's hand.

pretending that hee was driven to take up the £100 in gold he carryed to the King from Collonel Strangways upon his owne bond, and soe stood obliged to repay the same; whereas the latter asserted his being injured by that pretence of Sir Francis Windham's, for that hee had sent it in pure duty and loyalty to the King, as being all hee was then able to doe for him, and that the note which hee did indeed receive for it from Sir Francis Windham was only to secure himselfe against any danger he might be exposed to from his having supplyed the King this money, by being able from this pretended note to say that it was only so much money lent to Sir Francis Windham, in case the same should be extorted from or otherwise discovered by Sir Francis; appealing to him, the sayd Sir Francis, whither he had ever in so many yeares demanded, or so much as mentioned to him this note, or his reckoning it as a debt upon him. Which the other not being able to gainsay him in, my Lord Chancellor accommodated the businesse between them, so that there was noe more heard of it; but sattisfaction given to Collonel Strangwayes, by the King's owning his being abundantly convinced of the sincerity as well as seasonablenesse of that expression of his loyalty to him.

S. Pepys.[16]

Appendix

Extract from William Ellesdon's Narrative.

. . . . Upon or about the 18th of September 1651, the aforesaid honourable and truly loyal gentleman, Colonel Francis Wyndham, came to me at my house at Lyme (where I then lived, looking upon it as some protection to me in those times to live in that town), when, after some other discourse had, and an engagement to secresy passed betwixt us, he told me that the King had sent him to me, commanding me to procure him a vessel in order to his transportation into some part of France.

Being overjoyed to hear that my sovereign was so near me (as the Colonel had informed me he was), and even ravished with

[16] This document is in Pepys's own hand.

content that an opportunity of expressing the loyalty of my heart to his most excellent Majesty so unexpectedly presented itself, I answered that I would with the utmost hazard of my person, and whatsoever else was dear unto me (as knowing myself by all obligations, both sacred and civil, thereunto obliged), strenuously endeavour the execution of his Majesty's both just and reasonable commands in this particular, being verily persuaded that either God would preserve me from, or else support me in and under any sufferings for so good a cause. Accordingly, I immediately sent one to the custom-house to make enquiry who had entered his vessel as bound for France. News was brought me that one Stephen Limbry of Charmouth had lately entered his bark, and intended a speedy voyage for St. Malo.

Not only myself, but also Colonel Wyndham was much affected with these tidings; I having told him that I had an interest in the master (he being my tenant), and that he had ever the repute of being well affected to his Majesty. Upon these encouragements, we (resolving to lose no time) rode to Charmouth by the seaside to confer with the master; which way I the rather made choice of, that in our passage there I might show the colonel what place I judged most convenient for his Majesty to take boat in (in case we could work the master to a compliance), in order to his embarking. And, indeed, a more commodious place for such a design could hardly be found, it lying upon the shore a quarter of a mile from any house and from any horse or footpath. The Colonel being fully satisfied of the conveniency of the place, we rode into the town and immediately sent for the master, who, being very happily at home, presently repaired to us at the inn.

Friendly salutations and some endearing compliments being premised (and a name that was not his own [17] being by me, in the hearing of the master, given to the Colonel, in the way of disguise), I told him that the end of our sending for him was to procure passage for a friend of mine and this gentleman's, who had a finger in the pye at Worcester. The man being startled at this proposition (as apprehending more than ordinary danger in such an undertaking), we were necessitated to use many arguments for the removal of his fears; which we so happily managed, that in a little time we saw the effect of them by his chearful undertaking the business. Wherefore, an ample reward being engaged on for our part, he promised speedily to repare his vessel, and hale her out of the cob the Monday following, and about midnight to send his boat to the place appointed for the taking

[17] Captain Norris. according to Anne Wyndham.

in of the passenger, and then immediately to put off to sea (in case the winds were favourable). Thus far we were agreed; and in all our discourse, there was no enquiry made by the master, nor any the least intimation given by us, who this passenger might be, whose quality we purposely concealed, lest the hopes of gaining £1000 (the promised reward of the highest treason) might prove a temptation too strong for the master to grapple with.

Having thus far successfully proceeded in our business, we returned to Lyme. And the next day (being Friday), Colonel Wyndham resolved upon returning to his house at Trent with these hopeful tidings to his Majesty. I bore him company part of his journey, and chose the land road from Lyme to Charmouth, that upon the top of a hill, situate in our way betwixt these two towns, upon a second view he might be the more perfectly acquainted with the way that leads from Charmouth to the place appointed for his Majesty's taking boat—it being judged most convenient, upon several accounts, that the Colonel, and not myself, should be his Majesty's conductor thither. Here, calling to mind that on Monday (the day appointed for his Majesty's embarking) a fair was to be held at Lyme, and withal doubting lest upon that account (through the nearness of the place) our inn in Charmouth might be filled with other guests, we sent down one Harry Peters, then a servant of the Colonel's (who yet was not with us the day before), with instructions, by an earnest of five shillings, to secure the two best rooms in the inn against his Majesty's coming. Who told the hostess (to take off suspicion) this fair tale: that there was a young man to come thither the next Monday, that had stolen a gentlewoman to marry her, and (fearing they should be followed and hindered) that he desired to have the house and stables at liberty to depart at whatsoever hour of the night he should think fittest.

This message being performed, the rooms made sure of, and the servant returned, I then showed the Colonel a country house of my father's, distant both from Lyme and Charmouth about a mile and a half,[18] which (for the privacy of it) we determined should be the place whither his Majesty, with the Lord Wilmot, who then waited upon him, should repair on Monday next, that I might then and there give his Majesty a farther account of what had passed in the interim between myself and the master.

And now, being abundantly satisfied and exhilarated in the review of the happy progress we had thus far made, with most affectionate embraces the noble Colonel and myself parted; he

[18] At Wilde.

returning to his house to wait upon his Majesty, and myself towards
mine, vigorously to prosecute what yet remained on my part to be
done with the master, in order to the compleating of this work thus
happily begun. In the performance of which, that I might approve
myself faithful, I the same day, and the day following and also on the
Monday after, having diligently sought out the master, moved and
pressed him so earnestly to the punctual performance of his passed
promise, that he seemed discontented at my importunity, as betraying
in me a suspicion of his fidelity. A little to allay his passion, I told him
I was assured that the gentleman, my friend, would be at Charmouth
on Monday, and that if he were not ready to transport him, it might
prove an undoing both to my friend and me. Whereupon, to vindicate
himself, he told me that he had taken in his ballast, that he had
victualled himself, and haled out his vessel to the cob's mouth, for fear
of being beneaped, because the tides at that time were at the lowest.

Being well satisfied with this answer, I left him (after that I
had given him instructions how to prevent any jealousies that might
arise in the breasts of the mariners concerning the persons to be
transported), and immediately went to the aforesaid country house of
my father's. Whither when I was come (and perceived that I was the
first comer), that I might also erect a blind before the tenant's eyes, I
demanded of him whither the London carrier had passed that day or
not; telling him, withal, that I expected two or three friends, who
promised to meet me there about the time of the carrier's passing that
way.[19]

His answer to me was but little to the purpose; but in half an
hour after my arrival there, came the King, with Mrs. Julian
Coningsby, a kinswoman of the Colonel's, who rode behind him, the
Lord Wilmot, Colonel Wyndham and his man Peters attending on
him. After their coming in, I took the first opportunity to acquaint his
Majesty with what had passed betwixt myself and the master after
Colonel Wyndham's departure from me. The result of all which was
this: that the master had assured me that all things were in a readiness
for the intended voyage, and that (according to the instructions given
him) he had possessed the seamen with a belief that one of the
passengers—viz. my Lord Wilmot—was a merchant, by name Mr.
Payne; and the other, meaning the king, was his servant. That the
reason of Mr. Payne's taking ship at Charmouth at such an
unseasonable hour, and not at Lyme, was because that, being a town

[19] According to Abraham Poger, as reported through Alford, this
device did not deceive the tenant, and Poger dissuaded him from
informing only by insisting on the moral duties in the matter.

corporate, he feared an arrest, his factor in St. Malo having broken him in his estate by his unfaithfulness to him; and that therefore he was necessitated with this his servant speedily and privately to transport himself to St. Malo aforesaid, in order to the recovery of such goods of his as by his said factor were detained from him, the sending of which goods at several times this servant of his could sufficiently testify and prove. This I the rather acquainted his Majesty and the Lord Wilmot with, that after their being shipped (the more to confirm the mariners), they might drop some discourses to this effect.

His Majesty having showed his approbation of what I had done, was graciously pleased, as a testimony of his royal favour (which I have ever esteemed as a jewel of greatest worth), to bestow upon me a piece of gold, telling me that at present he had nothing to bestow upon me but that small piece; but that if it ever should please God to restore him to his kingdom, he would readily grant me whatever favour I might in reason petition him for.

Upon this, his Majesty, attended as is before expressed, rode towards Charmouth, commanding me to hasten to Lyme and there to continue my care that all things might be performed according to his Majesty's expectations and the master's promise. Accordingly, I made haste home, found out the master, acquainted him that my friend was now at Charmouth, and that I newly came from him. He replied that he was glad of it, that he would presently repair to Charmouth to speak with him, and to tell him when he would come ashore for him; which accordingly he did.

And thus far all things succeeded according to our best wishes, both the wind and tide seeming to be at strife which of them should most comply with our desires. But after all these fair hopes, and the great likelihood we had all conceived of his Majesty's happy transportation, it pleased God Almighty, for the clearer manifestation of his infinitely glorious wisdom and powerful goodness in his Majesty's preservation, suddenly to blast this design and to cast his Majesty upon new streights and dangers.

For the master, either through weakness of judgment, or else in design to prevent a discovery, had utterly forborne to acquaint his wife with his intentions to go to sea, until it was almost time for him to go abroad. Whereupon, he no sooner called for his chest, but his wife asked him why he would go to sea, having no goods aboard. The master now thought himself necessitated to tell her Mr. Ellesdon had provided him a fraught which would be much more worth to him than if his ship were full loaden with goods, he being to transport a gentleman, a friend of his. His wife (having been at Lyme Fair that day, and having heard the proclamation read, wherein £1000 was promised as a reward for the discovery of the king, and in which the danger of those also was represented that should conceal his Majesty or any of those that were engaged with him at Worcester, and apprehending that this gentlemen might be one of the party), forthwith locked the doors upon him, and by the help of her two daughters kept him in by force, telling him that she and her children would not be undone for ever a landlord of them all; and threatened him that if he did but offer to stir out of doors, she would instantly go to Lyme and give information both against him and his landlord to Captain Macy, who had then the command of a foot company there. Here the master showed his wisdom not a little by his peaceable behaviour; for had he striven in the least, it is more than probable his Majesty and his attendants had been suddenly seized upon in the inn.

But I must needs awhile leave the master a prisoner in his own house, his wife and daughters being now become his keepers, whilst I render an account of the actings of Colonel Wyndham, who, with his man Peters, at the time appointed went to the place agreed upon, to expect the landing of the boat. But no boat coming, after several hours waiting (because he saw the tide was spent), he resolved upon returning to the inn. In his way thither he discovers a man coming towards him, dogged at a small distance by two or three women. This, indeed, was the master of the vessel, who by this time had obtained liberty (yet still under the eyes of his over-jealous keepers) to walk towards the seaside, with an intention to make known to those that waited there for him the sad tidings of this unexpected disappointment, together with its causes. The Colonel (when they met), though he conceived it might be the master, yet, being not certain of it, and seeing the women at his heels, passed him by without enquiring into the non-performance of his promise.

Your lordship may easily guess that this frustration of hopes was matter of trouble as well as admiration to his Majesty. The issue of it was that Peters, very early the Tuesday morning, was sent unto me to know the reason of it. He had no sooner delivered his message but astonishment seized on me; and foresight of those sad consequences which I feared might be the fruits of this disaster wrought in me such disquietment of mind, that (for the time) I think I scarcely sustained the like upon any occasion in all my life before, my confidence of his Majesty's safe departure adding not a little to the weight of that load of sorrow which afterwards lay so heavy upon me. The cause, I plainly told him, I was wholly ignorant of, except this were it: that in regard it was Fair-day, the master might not be able effectually to command his mariners out of the alehouses to their work; but promised speedily to search into it. And upon enquiry, I found it to be what I have before related.[20]

[20] In briefer form, lacking some details and the incident of Wyndham's passing Limbry and the women on the beach, the same story is given by Anne Wyndham in 1667. She also states that Limbry, "under his own hand," gave this explanation of why he failed to appear.

～X～

ORIGINAL NOTES FROM COLONEL PHILLIPS

Colonel Robert Phillips's "Notes" appear in two texts in the collection
—one in his own hand, the other a copy made by the clerk who
transcribed several other documents in the collection. The latter copy
is followed by a number of blank leaves, and it may have been meant
for use in an interview with the Colonel similar to the one that Pepys
had with Father Huddlestone. The alterations in the original copy are
in Phillips' hand and there is no evidence that Pepys edited the
document.

A few extracts were printed as notes to Dalrymple's edition of
the King's narrative, and Alexander M. Broadley, *The Royal Miracle*
(London, 1912), prints the text of "the original manuscript."

This narrative was the first of the supporting stories that Pepys
collected: he refers to it in his letter to the Duke of York of June 6,
1681, and so he must have acquired it some time between then and
the preceding October 5.

The Colonel relates his part in the events of September 24 to
October 15, the period when the King was attempting to get passage
to France from some Hampshire or Sussex port.

COLL. PHILLIPP'S NOTES

On Thursday the 24th [1] of September, 1651, the then Lord Wilmott (afterward Earle of Rochester) was sent by his Majestie from Trent in Sommersetshire, the house of Coll. Francis Wyndham, to Salisbury, to Mr. Coventrye [2] and Coll. Robert Phelipps, which was occasioned by Mr. Edward Hyde's (brother-in-law to Coll. Francis Wyndham) discourse there at dinner the day before, who said that he had binn at Salisbury, where he saw his father Phelipps (for soe he usually called him) returned to his family, and that he was permitted by the Committee to remaine soe (the unfortunate business of Worcester having at present quieted theire feares and jealousies). [3]

My Lord, at his arrivall to the Kings Armes Inn, then kept by a harty Cavalier, Mr. Henry Hewett, sent first to Mr. John Coventrye, to whom my Lord discoursed his errand. [4] And then Mr. Coventrye sent for Coll. Phelipps, who presently came; and after my Lord and he had saluted, they having bin formerly acquainted in the armie, Mr. Coventrye left them together, saying he would goe into the next roome and take a pipe of tobaco with Mr. Hewett. Then my Lord asked the Collonel whether hee could helpe a gentleman in distress out of the kingdome.

The Collonel answered he would willingly give him the best directions he could, it being a duty every gentleman owed another in such circumstances, but was reserved enough (having heard before that that Lord had too warmly ingaged himselfe with Arguile's faction in Scotland); which the Lord quickly perceiving, told him: "Sir, I am commanded to be free with you, and to let you know that the King is at Coll. Wyndham's house at Trent, and his condition is such that he knows not how to dispose

[1] Replacing "25." Thursday, September 25th, was in fact correct. Phillips misdates events by one day throughout.

[2] John Coventry's role, which was important according to Phillips and Anne Wyndham, is unmentioned in the King's own narrative.

[3] This explanation is lacking in other reports.

[4] Blount says that Coventry lived in Salisbury Cathedral close.

of himselfe. He is assured of your fidelitie, and is told that noe man is more capable to serve him in this exigent. He therefore committs himselfe to your care to provide for his safety."

At which discourse the Collonel was not a little amazed, and could not undertake soe difficult a province without great apprehension of what might not only possibly, but even probably (as things then stood) unfortunately fall out. But then on the other hand, considering that it was a riske which must be ventered on, or the king be lost, he told the Lord that he would undertake it, assuring him that if the King miscarried in his hands, the willing sacrificing of his owne life should beare testimonie of his truth and sinceritie.

Then came in Mr. Coventry, and said, "Well gentlemen are you agreed?" Both answered, "Yeas." Then after drinking a bottle or two of wine and hearing my Lord discourse of theire adventures since Worcester fight, Mr. Coventry and the Collonel tooke theire leaves. And as they went along the Close, the Collonel acquainted Mr. Coventrye with what had past betweene the Lord and him; and Mr. Coventry was glad that the Collonel had undertaken it, and wished him good lucke, assuring him that he would assist in anything within his power.

Soe they parted to their severall homes. And the next morning early, the Collonel went to Southampton to one Mr. Horne, a marchant of very good creditt in that towne and a very good acquaintance of the Collonel's. But he being out of towne, and intending to returne home the next day, the Collonel left a letter for him importing that he had earnest bussiness to speake with him, and that he was only gonn to Collonel St. Barbes house, 6 myles from Southampton, whither he desired Mr. Horne to come to him the next day if he returned home time enough. Mr. Horne, returning home next morning, was so freindly as presently to come to Collonel St. Barbe's, where he found them at dinner. After they had dined, Collonel [5] Phelipps and Mr. Horne walked into the garden. The Collonel told him that he had occasion of a barke to carry him and a freind or two into France. Mr. Horne, after some pause, answered, "There is such a man now at home,

[5] Replacing "the Collonel."

soe honest a fellow that I would trust tenn thousand lives, were I
master of as many, in his hands; and I will make hast home and
speake with him."

Soe Mr. Horne departed, and appointed the Collonel to
meet him and the master of the barke the next day, being Sunday,
at 3 of the clock in the afternoon at Redbridge. They all
accordingly meet at the place and time appointed, where Mr.
Horne quickly made an agreement betweene the Collonel and the
master of the barke, which was 40*li*. The barke being on shoare,
the master desired some mony in hand to provide his vessell, men
and provisions. The Collonel then gave him 20*li*., and the master
promised to bee ready on Wensday night, on [6] which day the
Collonel promised to come to the Beare Inn, without the gate at
Southampton, to receive an account.

He accordingly came thither, sent to Mr. Horne into the
towne, who came with the master of the barke with [7] him, and
they acquainted the Collonel with the sad event of this essay,
which was that his barke was pressed to carry provisions to the
fleet which then lay before Jersey under the command of Generall
Blake. The honest master of the barke returned 10*li* to the
Collonel of his impress mony; and the Collonel and Mr. Horne
thought it unsafe to make any new [8] attempt in that place.

Soe the Collonel returned to Salisbury, where upon advise
with Mr. Coventrye and Dr. Henchman (afterward Byshop of
London), 'twas resolved to try the Sussex coast; and to that
purpose the Collonel proposed to make use of the interest of his
very good freind, the faythfull and loyall Collonell Gunter, who
lived nere Chichester, which was approved (Collonel Gunter
being very well knowen to the Reverend Doctor). Whereupon,
Coll. Phelipps writes his letter to Coll. Gunter, and the Doctor
another: which letters were dispatched to him by the safe hands
of Mr. Hyde, a loyall sequestred minister. And in the interim,
whilest Coll. Gunter was acting his part to provide the vessell,
Coll. Phelipps went downe to Trent to fetch the King from
thence.

[6] Replacing "at."
[7] Replacing "to."
[8] Replacing "more."

Thither he came on the 4th of October, being Sunday; and the next morning, the King, with Mrs. Conisby behind him (the same who rid behind his Majestie formerly to Lyme) and Henry Peeters, servant to Coll. Wyndham, went under the conduct of Coll. Phelipps in private ways (all that country being very well knowen to him) [9] nere 40 myles that day to the house of the Widdow Hyde at Hele, 3 myles distant from Salisbury, a very discreet gentlewoman. Hither was Dr. Henchman come before from Salisbury to provide for theire reception.

Hence, the next morning, the King and Coll. Phelipps seemingly went away, rid about the Downes, and tooke a veiw of the wonder of that country, Stonheng,[10] where they found that the King's Arithmaticke gave the lye to that fabulous tale that those stones cannot be told alike twice together. But this ariseing [11] was the effect rather of convenience then curiositie, for that day being a faire at Salisbury, Mistris Hyde gave leave to all her servants to goe thither, whilest the [12] King, who went away in theire sight with Coll. Phelipps in the morning, after his toure taken about the Downes, returned to Hele againe that afternoone in theire absence. That morning Mistris Conisby and Harry Peeters returned homeward alsoe.

The same afternoon Coll. Phelipps, having safely delivered the King into the hands of Dr. Henchman in the feild nere Hele, went that evening (leading the horse the King rode on) to his most faythfull friend Mr. Jones his house at Newton-Tony. Thence early in the morning he tooke his journey towards Coll. Gunters, to see what success he had had in his negotiation; which he to his noe smal satisfaction found to have binn prosperous, for by the meanes of a kinsman of his, Mr. Thomas Gunter, a prudent loyal gentleman, and one Mr. Francis Mansell, a faythfull marchant, Captaine Tettershall was provided to be ready with his barke nere Brighthempson, towards Shoram, on Tuesday the 13th of October at night, to take in his designed Royall freight.

[9] Replacing "the Coll."
[10] Replacing "Stonnage."
[11] Manuscript "areiring." The duplicate copy gives the reading printed here.
[12] Replacing "Coll. P."

With which joyfull news, Coll. Phelipps returned on the 11th of October to Salisbury. The same evening, Dr. Henchman went to Hele to give notice of the success and to prepare the King to bee ready at the meadow-gate opening into the river, where Coll. Phelipps would bee by three of the clock in the morning with a leade-horse for the King. Accordingly, the Collonel came to the place at the time appointed, but had the misfortune to have the King's horse, at the entring of the meadow-gate, to breake his bridle and run upp the river—which, after some short [13] time, with noe smal trouble, he recovered and brought back. And having in some tolerable manner amended what had bin broken, the King and the Collonel sett forward for Brighthempson, and that afternoone, nere Hamilton in Hampshire, they meet with Coll. Gunter and his [14] kinsman Mr. Thomas Gunter, who carried the [15] company to one Mr. Simonds his house, who had married the sister of Coll. Gunter, a most harty loyall gentlewoman, where they were kindly treated. Hither alsoe came the Lord Wilmott and Robert Swan his then servant.

On the next morning early, they began theire journey to Brighthempson, where they all arrived safe that night; only Coll. Phelipps, who left them that day and went by the King's command (procured by the Lord Wilmott) to London to provide some mony to meet the King at Rouen.

This night, the King was knowen by the inn-keeper at Brighthempson, who had bin one of his father's guard; but he proved faythfull, and serviseable too.

About 3 of the clock the next morning, the King, and Lord Wilmot only, tooke [16] shipping betweene Brighthempson and Shoram, and happily landed in a short time at [Fécamp [17]] some few leauges from Deipe in Normandy, whence they went to Rouen, where Coll. Phelipps' letters from London with a bill of exchange meet them.

Coll. Gunter came immediatly to London, where he found

---

[13] Replacing "smal."
[14] Replacing "Mr."
[15] Replacing "us."
[16] Replacing "and Lord Wilmot."
[17] Name is blank in the manuscript.

Coll. Phelipps out; and he complaining that some whom he had imployed expected some moneys presently, Coll.[18] Phelipps did furnish him with 50*li* in gold and 50*li* in silver, which monys Mr. John Coventrye repayed at Coll. Phelipps his returne to Salisbury.[19]

[18] Replacing "he."
[19] This report is endorsed: "Colonell Philips his Notes, relateing to his Majesty's Escape from Worcester."

~XI~

COLONEL GOUNTER'S REPORT

Pepys acquired Colonel George Gounter's narrative after he had had
the rest of his collection bound, and he therefore put it with other
manuscripts, which were later bound and labelled *Miscellaneous*: the
error on his Table of Contents and in his catalogue, of stating that it
was in Volume IX of the series of printed documents that he labelled
Consutilia, may have arisen from their being shelved in the same press
with the *Miscellaneous* volume. Pepys's main collection of documents
relating to the King's escape was completed in December, 1684. The
Gounter narrative is placed in the *Miscellaneous* volume just before a
copy of Sir Lionel Jenkins's will of July 21, 1685. It appears,
therefore, to have come into Pepys's hands early in 1685, shortly after
his main collection was bound.

      Three manuscripts of this narrative have survived. One, now a
Tanner Manuscript in the Bodleian Library, is an early-eighteenth-
century copy of Pepys's manuscript. It seems to have been known by
the editors of the 1725 edition of Thomas Blount's *Boscobel*, but its
only publication is in Henry Cary's *Memorials of the Great Civil War
in England* (London, 1842). The second manuscript is now Additional manuscript 9008 in the British Museum. It was purchased from
a Mr. Bartlett of Havant, who found it in a secret drawer of an old
cabinet he bought when the Gounter home at Racton in Sussex was
pulled down in 1830. It was first published in J. D. Parry, *An
Historical and Descriptive Account of Sussex* (Brighton, 1833); a
separate edition appeared as *The Last Act in the Miraculous Story of
His Majesty's Escape* (London, 1846), and it is also included in Allan

Fea's *The Flight of the King* (London, 1904). The third manuscript
is the item in Manuscript 2099 in the Pepysian Library.

The Racton and Pepysian copies are written in the same
seventeenth-century hand. The Racton copy has numerous changes in
two hands. One is that of the main copyist, who restores in the
margins and between lines a few words and phrases that had been
accidentally omitted in copying—these corrections produce the same
readings as in the Pepysian copy. The second hand is that of a
seventeenth-century editor, who altered phrases, made the presentation consistently third-person, changed words to produce greater
clarity, added several small details, and continued the title with the
words, "as itt was taken from his mouth by a person of worth a little
before his death." This editor therefore had special knowledge of
Colonel Gounter, the local situation, and the events recorded in the
narrative. Pepys's manuscript, on the other hand, is a very clean copy:
apart from one small omission, the only changes are one minor
replacement and two alterations, all in the hand of the editor of the
Racton copy and all producing readings that make the two copies
agree.

The date and place of Colonel Gounter's death does not
appear in English records; but from a grant made to his widow, it must
have occurred in 1661 or before, and probably abroad. From this, it
would seem that his narrative was taken down abroad just before he
died, and was sent to England to his family, who saw two copies of it
made at one time. One of these manuscripts was edited, possibly by
some member of the family; the other ultimately came to Samuel
Pepys, in the early part of 1685.

The Pepysian manuscript, which provides the base-text for the
present edition, is therefore the copy that is closest to the lost original.
Changes made by the editor of the Racton copy are here presented in
an appended note. These changes were adopted in Parry's text but
ignored in the 1846 and later editions.

The narrative deals with the last week of the King's
adventures, October 6–16, the period in which Colonel Gounter made
several attempts to get the King shipping from Hampshire and Sussex
ports and finally succeeded in setting him off from Shoreham.

> *The last act in the miraculous storie of his Majes-
> tie's escape: being a true and perfect relation of his
> conveyance through many obstacles, and after many
> dangers, to a safe harbour, out of the reach of his*

*tyrannicall ennemies: by Colonell Gounter, of
Rackton in Sussex, whoe had the happines to bee
instrumentall in the busines.*[1]

The King was now att Heale,
within three miles of Salisbury, where wee begin our storie.
My Lord Willmot, his faithfull and watchfull attendant, at
Salisburie. There, Dr. Hinchman, now Right Revd. Bishop of
Salisburie (inspired by God himselfe, as may well be thought by
the successe) gave him counsell, first to try at Laurence Hydes,
Esquire, living at Hinton Daubnay in Hampshire, neere the seaside, what could bee done for a passage: then, if that did not
succeed, to repaire to Col. George Gounter, at Rackton, fower
miles from Chichester in Sussex; being verie confident of his
fidelitie, and that he would contribute to the utmost of his power
to bring this great and weightie busines, as for the difficulties they
must encounter, soe for the consequence of the issue, to a good
end.

Here, before I proceed in the storie, the reader will give
mee leave to putt him in mind, that wee write not an ordinarie
storie, where the reader, engaged by noe other interest than
curiositie, may soone be cloyed with circumstances which signifye
no more unto him but that the author was at good leasure and
was very confident of his readers patience. In the relation of
miracles, every petty circumstance is materiall and may affoord to
the judicious reader matter of good speculation: of such a miracle
especially, where the restoration of noe lesse then three kingdomes, and his owne particular safety and libertie (if a good and
faithfull subject) was att the stake.

I may not therefore omitt to lett him knowe how things
stood with the Colonell att that tyme when this resolution (which
prooved happy in the successe) was taken. Not above fourteene
dayes before, the said Colonell Gounter was confyned, upon

---

[1] The page is headed in another hand "By Coll. Gunter"; and in
the top margin is a note by O. F. Moreshead, "This is a transcript of Brit.
Mus. Add. MS. 9008. O.F.M. 1926."

paine of imprisonment, not to stirre five miles from home. In the
very nick of tyme, when he was first thought upon for soe great a
worke, comes a messenger, with a warrant from the Commissioners of Haberdashers Hall, London, to summon him to appeare
before them within ten dayes, to pay twoe hundred pounds for his
fifth-and-twentieth part which they had sett him, upon payne of
sequestration on default. Hee first refused, and told the messenger
that he was confined and could not goe five miles from home. But
he left with him the order, and told him it should be at his perill
if he did not obey it.

The Colonel the next day repaired to Chichester, fower
miles from him, to the Commissioners there, to shew them his
order. They peremptorily replyed, he must goe, and his orders
would beare him out. Hee went accordingly, and compounded
with them, and gott of 100*li* of the twoe hundred he was sett att.
But his creditt being shaken, the currant running then soe hard
against the King, the royall party, and all good men, that hee
could not borrow the money in all London, he was forced with all
speede to repaire into the countrey, and went privatly to his
usurer, whoe had the securitie of his whole estate. Hee shewed
him his danger, and requested to borrowe a hundred pounds,
upon his bond and his former securitie; whoe readily conde-
scended, and told him out the money. The next day hee was to
call for it and seale the bond.

Hee had noe sooner ended this busines, being stayed some
whatt longer by some friends then he intended, but that very
night he came home (being 7 October, 1651.),
hee found some att his house, whoe were come
about this designe. I thinck it will easily be
graunted by any that reades and considers, that this was not without a providence, since that it is apparent that if his friends had
come before he had beene licenced to goe abroad, he must needs
have beene excused: and if they had come much after, it was possible a new restraint might have come betweene, or his libertie in
goeing soe freely up and downe, after his busines ended, more
suspected. But now to the storie and entertainment of his guests.

Betwixt eight and nine of the clock at night, the Colonel
came home. Entring in att his doore, the Colonel's ladye mett him
and told him there was in the parlour a Deavonshire gentleman

sent by Mr. Hyde aforesaid about a reference, "which none besydes yourselfe can decyde." At the Colonel's coming in, he found his Devonshire gentleman setting at one end of the chimney, Captaine Thomas Gounter att the other, and his lady (which was gone in before) in the middle. The gentleman rose and saluted him.

The Colonel presently knew him to bee the Lord Wilmot. Which the noble Lord perceyving, tooke the Colonel asyde to the windowe: "I see you know mee (said he); do not owne mee." Captaine Thomas Gounter, the Colonel's kinsman, for all he had a long tyme beene in the army and under his command, knewe him not; which was strange, the noble Lord beeing but meanely disguised.

After a bottle of sack, which afforded some matter of discourse by reason of twoe waspes, or rather hornetts, which came out at the opening, a short collation being made readie as soon as could [be] (his lady having given leave to her servants to bee from home that day): my Lords man, one Swan, comming in to waite, whispered his master in the eare and told him my Lord Wentworth's boy Ponie was without, and wished him to be carefull, for feare the boy should knowe him, being taken by Captaine Thomas Gounter in distresse att Chelsey, and cloathed by him to wayte upon him.

Supper ended, there was whispering betwixt the Colonel's kinsman and his lady, and shee told him shee was confident of a disguise, and that it was the Maister, by his hand. He beat her of of it as much as hee could, suspecting noe such matter himselfe.

Within halfe an hower after supper, the Colonel offerd the noble Lord, then by name Mr. Barlowe, it beeing late, and as the greatest courtesie he could then shewe him, to waite upon him to his chamber and to bedd, which he readily accepted. The Colonel tooke up the candle, the noble Lord following him, his lady and kinsman attending. When he came into the chamber, it being late, the Colonel desired his lady and kinsman to goe to bedd, and to leave him, for he was bound to waite upon this gentleman a whyle. They tooke leave, and bidd him good night.

The noble Lord and Colonel being alone, he broke the busines unto the Colonel with these words, sighing: "The King of

England, my maister, your maister, and the maister of all good Englishmen, is neere you, and in great distresse. Can you helpe us to a boate?" The Colonel, looking very sadly, after some pause said, "Is he well? Is hee safe?" He said, "Yeas." The Colonel replyed, "God be blessed," and gave him a reason for his question: if he should not bee secure, hee doubted not but hee could secure him till a boate could be gotten.

The noble Lord, not knowing what had beene done, and what course had been taken for securing of his Majestie at Heale since he came away, answered the Colonel hee hoped he was out of daunger at present, but intended to bee at his house with him on the Wendsday. Soe he said, and soe it seemes it was resolved; but second thoughts, and unexpected accommodations elsewhere, had altered the designe. However, upon the hearing of this, the Colonel's thoughts were much raised in expectation of such a guest, untill he was better informed, as hee was soone after to his good content and satisfaction, knowing the house well and the conveniences thereof, and the worth and fidelitie of the persons.[2]

Now to the maine busines of procuring a boate. The Colonel told the Lord seriously, and nothing but the trueth, that for all he lived so neere the sea, yet there was noe man living soe little acquainted with those kind of men. However, as he thought himselfe bound by all obligations, sacred and civill, to doe his utmost to preserve his King, soe hee would faithfully promise with all possible care and alacritie, yea expedition (which he accounted to bee the life of such a busines), to acquitt himselfe of his dutie. The noble Lord, my honoured friend (ô that God had beene pleased to have spared him life) was aboundantly satisfyed with this answer, hugging him in his armes, and kist his cheeke againe and againe.

For that tyme the Colonel bidd him good-night, desiring him to rest secure, for that he would watch whilest he slept, and that he doubted not butt in good tyme all would bee well. Comming into his chamber, he found his wyfe had stayed up for him, and was verie earnest to knowe whoe this was and what was his busines.

[2] According to Blaauw, the original plan was that the King should hide at Racton while a vessel was procured at Emsworth.

The Colonel desired her to excuse him, assuring her it was nothing concerning her, or that would any-wayes damnifie her. Shee was confident there was more in it then soe, and enough, shee doubted, to ruine him and all his family. "And in that," said shee, "I am concerned," breaking out into very great passion of weeping.

Which the Colonel seeing, tooke a candle, pretending to goe into the next roome; but privately to my Lord Wilmot and acquainted him how it was, asking his advice whether, as the case stood, it were any way amisse to acquaint her with it. That he durst passe his word for the loyaltie and integritye of his wife of his wife: however, without his allowance, shee should knowe nothing. The noble Lord replyed, "No, no, by all meanes acquaint her with it." I humbly thancked him, and bidd him goodnight againe.

The Colonel comming in to his chamber, unfolded the busines, wyped the teares of his ladyes eyes, whoe, smiling, said, "Goe on, and prosper. Yet I feare you will hardly doe it." "However," said the Colonel, "I must endeavour, and will doe my best, leaving the successe to God allmightie"; his lady deporting herselfe, during the whole carriage of the busines, with soe much discretion, courage, and fidelitie, that (without vanitie bee it spoken) shee seemed (her danger considerd) to outgoe her sexe. Neyther will the reader thinck this an impertinant circumstance, since the successe of the busines did not a little depend of her concurrence.

The Colonel, contenting himselfe with very little sleepe that night, rose very early the next morning, being Wednesday, the 8th of Octobre, as he had promised the Lord Wilmot, and rode to Emsworth, a place twoe miles from him and by the sea side, passing through Boorne. Hee tooke an old servant of his formerly, John Day, a trustie man and verie loyall subject, whoe was related to seamen of very good accoumpt whoe with their barkes used to lye there. But they being out of the way, could doe noe good there, although fower yeares after, the Colonel did at the same place at his owne charges hire a barke for the Lord Wilmot, whoe came over att his Majestie's command, and loosing his designe was forced to come from allmost the furthest North to the South before hee could gett

8 October

a passage. Soe few friends then had his Sacred Majestie in his distresses, now soe numerous in expectation of rewards.

The Colonel hasted all he could home, to give my Lord accoumpt, whoe had promised not to stirre till the Colonell came: but being impatient of any delay, had left the Colonells house, soe that the Colonel mett him within halfe a mile of it, and gave him an accoumpt of his mornings worke, that nothing could be done where he had beene.

The noble Lord and the Colonel rid on, and went to Langstone, a place by the sea, and where boates use. As he was riding along, he putt his hand in his pockett and missed his money, for comming away in hast from the Colonel's house, he had left it behinde him in his bedd. Immediatly, he sent his man Swan [3] for it. The Colonels ladye, hearing my Lord was gone, which shee much wonderd att, had beene in his chamber and found the bedd open, and in the middle a black purse full of gold, which shee had secured and gave it the man when he came for it.

When wee came to Langston, wee attempted all wee could, but in vaine. The noble Lord and the Colonel eate oisters there, and then they parted, the noble Lord to Mr. Hydes house aforesaid, there to expect the accoumpt of the Colonel's proceedings, the Colonel home and immediatly imployed his kinsman Captaine Thomas Gounter (whoe by this was made acquainted) to inquire of severall other places and to meete the Colonel next day att Chichester, to give him an accoumpt—all which the Colonel imparted that night to my Lord Willmot att Mr. Hyde's house at Hinton Daubney aforesaid.

After supper, the Colonel tooke his leave of the Lord, it being a very dismall night for winde and raine, which made the Lord very much to importune the Colonel to stay. But he refused, replying that delayes were dangerous; and lett the weather be what it would, he had a sure guide. The Colonel touched att his owne house by the way, betwixt one and twoe of the clock that night, and layd downe upon his bedd; and after twoe houres rest, rose from bedd and went immediatly to Chichester to meete his kinsman, Captaine Thomas Gounter (8th of Octobre) according to appointment. From whome he received this accoumpt: that

[3] Manuscript "Swant."

both he and his kinsman Mr. William Rishton, a loyall gentleman and one engaged all along in the warre under the Colonel's command, had endeavoured all they could, but without successe.

Then the Colonel bethought himselfe, and conceyved the next and best expedient would be to treate with a French marchant, one that usually traded into France; and went to one Mr. Francis Mançell, a stranger then to the Colonel and only knowen unto him by name, as casually he had mett him with severall other companies, pretending to give him a visitt and to be better acquainted with him. He received him courteously, and enterteined him with a bottle or twoe of his French wine and Spanish tobacco.

After a whyle, the Colonel broke the busines to him, saying, "I doe not only come to visitt you, but must request one favour of you." He replyed, "Anything in his power." Then the Colonel asked him if he could fraught a barke; "for," said he, "I have twoe speciall friends of mine, that have been engaged in a duell; and there is mischief done, and I am obliged to gett them of if I can."

Hee doubted not but he could, att such a place att Brightemston in Sussex. The Colonel prest him then to goe with him immediatly, and if he could effect the busines, he would give him fifty pounds for his peynes. But it beeing *slowe faire* [4] day there, and his partner out of the way, he could not possibly untill the next day, and then, he promised him faithfully, he would goe with him and doe his best. Soe accordingly wee agreed.

Then the Colonel, whoe had promised the noble Lord Willmot an accoumpt att Mr. Hyde's house aforesaid once in 12 or 24 houres att the furthest, repaired thither accordingly and told him all was done. The noble Lord approoved, and like the way wondrous well.

It being very late, and very darke and boistrous weather, the Colonel tooke his leave. His horse being allmost spent, borrowed a horse of his kinsman Mr. Hide, who lent him his faulkners horse, being, as it seemes, the best he then had; which served to carrie him home, and the next morning to Chichester.

[4] Sloe Fair.

The Colonel tooke his owne house in the way and rested
upon a bedd for a whyle, and went unto Chichester
the 10th of October, being Fryday, according to
former appointment. The marchant being destitute
of a horse, the Colonel horst him upon the horse borrowed of Mr.
Hyde, and borrowed one for himselfe of his kinsman, Captaine
Thomas Gounter, and went away accordingly, desiring his kinsman to repaire to my Lord Wilmot and to give him the accoumpt
of his departure from Chichester in further prosecution of the
busines and to remaine with him, in order to his commands during
his absence.

10 Oct.
Fryday

    Wee arrived to [5] Brighthemston [6] by twoe of the clock that
day. The marchant went immediatly to inquire: but the seaman
he chiefly depended upon was gone for Chichester, whoe had
bargained for a frought [7] there. But as Providence would have it,
he touched att Shoram, fower miles from Brighthemston. I perswaded the marchant to send to him immediatly to come to him
upon earnest busines; and I doubted not but he would come,
which tooke effect accordingly. The Colonel had agreed with the
marchant to treate with the boateman, being his affaire and trade
—he to sett by as newter, promising the marchant to make good
and to pay him whate're he should agree for; but withall desired
to gett it as low as he could.

    Wee stayed there that night, and by Saturday the 11th of
October, by twoe of the clock, made a parfect agreement, which was that he was to have 60*li* paid him
in hand, before hee tooke them into the boate.
More,[8] he would knowe what he should carrie, or he would not
treate. Soe that the marchant was forced to tell him, himselfe
knowing noe more then what the Colonel had said to him of twoe
friends, etc. He was to bee in readines upon an hower's warning;
and the marchant to stay there under pretence of fraughting his
barke, to see all things in readines against the Colonel and his
twoe friends arrival. For the Colonel knew not when he should
come, but privatly promised the marchant to defray all his

11 Oct.
Sat.

    [5] I.e., "at."
    [6] I.e., Brighton.
    [7] I.e., "freight."
    [8] Manuscript "For."

charges, and to give him fifty pounds as aforesaid for his peynes; which was afterwards accordingly done. But this 50*li,* and the 60*li* paid to the boateman, the King himselfe, before he went away, tooke order for, and his order was executed.

All things agreed upon, the Colonel tooke leave of the marchant about 3 of the clock, with all expedition to give my Lord Wilmot this account, and came to Mr. Hydes house aforesaid betwixt eight and nine in the night. But my Lord and the Colonel's kinsman, Captaine Gounter, were remooved to a tenant's of my Cozin Hyde's, one Mr. Browne, and one that had married my Cozin Gounters sister. But the Colonel, comming in att his Cozin Hyde's house as aforesaid, found there his Cozin Hyde, and Colonell Robert Philips in his chamber goeing to bedd, whoe was very inquisitive to knowe how things stood.

He gave [reply] in short, that all things were well and in a readines. Upon which, the noble Colonel Philipps replyed, "Thou shalt bee a sainct in my almanack for ever." Mr. Hyde was very earnest to have had the Colonel stay all night and to goe and give an account the morrow morning; but he desired to bee excused, for that he knew he was expected, and could not in honour but give his account without delay. Whereupon Colonel Philipps would goe with mee; and wee tooke leave of my Cozin Hyde for that night, and came where my Lord Wilmot was, and had earnestly expected mee. After I had saluted him and given him a full account of all proceedings, the noble Lord was infinitly pleased and satisfyed, and presently had in consultation whoe should goe for the King; and it was agreed that Colonel Philipps should, by reason that Colonel Gounter was much tyred, and would need rest for further imployement.

Soe Colonel Philipps, upon Sunday the 12th of Octobre, went to give the King an accoumpt, and to conduct
12 *Oct.*   him to the Lord Wilmot and to the said Colonel Gounter. In the interim, whylest they expected, upon Munday the 13th of October, the Lord Will-
13 *Oct.*   mot, Colonel Gounter and Captaine Thomas Gounter, being alltogether att dinner, agreed to ride out upon the Downes. The Colonel, for a blinde, went to Hamble-don, hard by, to give his sister a visitt, and there borrowed a brace of grey-hounds, for that his Cozin Gounter and other gentlemen

were upon the Downes and had a mind to have a course att a
haire. And 'twas possible, if they did not beate to farre and should
stay out late, they might all come and bee merry with her that
night. However, shee should be sure of her doggs. "If you doe,
you shall be heartily wellcome," was her answer.

The Colonel brought the greyhounds, and beate with my
Lord and his cozin untill his tyme served, and then left them,
resolving to ride untill he mett the King. And just as he came to
Warneford townes-end from old Winchester, he mett Colonel
Philipps conducting the King. Being neere the houses, the
Colonel ridd by them and tooke noe notice, went to an inne in
the towne, called for some beere and tooke a pipe, and stayed soe
long, that they were atopp old Winchester before he overtooke
them.

When he had overtaken them and done his dutie to his
Majestie, he directed them the safest way, and he would ride
before to finde out my Lord Wilmot. Which being done, wee all
came together. The King and my Lord had some private discourse
together. When wee came to Brawde-Halfe-penny, a little above
Hambledon, there the King spake to the Colonel: "Canst thou
gett mee a lodging hereabout?" The Colonel told him that his
Cozin Hyde's house aforesaid was taken up for him and was very
convenient, beeing neere and in the way.[9] But whether his
Majestie thought it to publick a place, or for what other reason I
know not, hee said, "Know you noe other?" "Yeas, may it please
your Majestie, I know divers yeomanly men where for a night
wee may be wellcome. And here is one whoe married my sister,
whose house stands privatly and out of the way." "Lett us goe
thither," [10] said the King.

Whylest wee were consulting this affaire, Captaine
Thomas Gounter, the Colonel's kinsman, and Swan, my Lord
Wilmot's man, ridd scouting about [11] Broade-Halfe-penny afore-
said, the Colonel conducting the King, my Lord Wilmot, and

---

[9] Blount says that Laurence Hyde and Thomas Henslow had both
provided secure lodging, and that the King chose Symonds's chiefly
because it lay more directly in the way to Brighton. The escape route
through Sussex was the same that Charles I intended to have taken had he
escaped from Carisbrook (Ludlow's *Memoirs*).

[10] Altered from "saith."

[11] Replacing "abroad."

Colonel Robert Philipps to his sisters house, a private way and
the backside of Hambledon, it being but halfe a mile from the
place aforesaid.

Alighting att the doore, the Colonel lead them in, the Lord
Wilmot following, the King putting Colonell Robert Philipps
before him, saying, "Thou lookest the most like a gentleman
now." Comming in, the Colonel's sister mett him. Wee all saluted
her. Shee brought us into a little parlour, where was a good fire.
This was about candle-lighting. Wine, ale, and biskets were
presently sett before us, with a very cheerefull countenance, as
though the Kings presence had had some secret influence upon
her, whoe suspected nothing lesse then that a king was present.

In an hower's space wee went to supper, being all sett
promiscuously att a round table: and having halfe-supt, in comes
the Colonel's sister's husband, Mr. Thomas Symones, whoe, as it
plainly appeared, had been in company that day. "This is brave,"
said he, "A man can noe sooner be out of the way, but his house
must be taken up with I know not whome." And looking in the
Colonel's face, "Is it you?" (said he) "you are wellcome; and, as
your friends, soe they are all." Passing round the table, and
viewing all the companie, he said, "These are all Hydes now."
But peeping in the King's face, said of him, "Heer's a Round-
head"; and addressing his speech to the Colonel, said, "I never
knew you keepe Round-heads' company before." To which the
Colonel replyed, " 'Tis noe matter; he is my friend and, I will
assure you, no daungerous man." Att which words, he clapt
himselfe downe in a chaire next the King, and tooke him by the
hand, shaking him, and saying, "Brother Roundhead, for his sake
thou art wellcome," all the whyle beleaving the King to bee soe
indeede, and making himselfe (whether for feare or in courtesie)
to bee one too, as well as he could act it, the King all the whyle
complying with him, to all our admirations. Now and then he
would sweare before he was aware, for which the King reprooved
him, "O deare brother, that is a 'scape: sweare not, I beseech you."
Nevertheles, in that humor he was, hee plyed us hard with strong
waters and beare, the King not knowing well how to avoid it but
as somebody or other, when he lookt asyde, would take it out of
his hand.

Supper being ended, it beeing tenn of the clock, the

Colonel began to bethinck himselfe that the King had ridd neere fourty myles that day, and was to undergoe a very hard journey the next; and how to gett the King out of his company and to bedd, hee could hardly devise. Yet the Colonel whispered his kinsman in the eare, saying, "I wonder how thou shouldest judge soe right; hee is a Round-head indeede, and if wee could gett him to bedd, the house were our owne, and wee could bee merry." Hee readily submitted, and the Colonel presently (leaving the Lord Wilmot behinde) conducted the King and Colonel Rob. Philips (whoe lay in the Kings chamber) to bedd.

The King slept well all night; and by breake of day, the Colonel putting up twoe neats-tongues [12] in his pocketts, which he thought they might neede by the way, they sett out and begun their journey.[13] They were noe sooner come to Arundell hill, as they rode close by the castle, but the Governour, Captaine Morley, mett them full-but, hunting. The Colonel, the better to avoid them, it beeing a steepe hill they were to goe downe, presently alighted, and his company (as was agreed before) did as he did, and soe happily they escaped them. The King being told whoe it was, replyed merrily: *"I did not like his starched mouchates."*

Soe wee came to Howton, where on horseback wee made a stopp at an ale-house for some bread and drinck; and there our neats-tongues stood us in very good steede, and were heartily eaten. From thence, being come to Bramber, wee found the streetes full of soldiers, on both sydes the houses, whoe unluckily, and unknowen to mee, were come thither the night before to guard. But luckily (or rather, by a very speciall providence) were just then come from their guard at [14] Bramber-bridge into the towne for refreshment. Wee came upon them unawares, and were seene before wee suspected any thing. My Lord Wilmot was readie to turne back, when I stept in and said: "If wee doe, wee are undone. Lett us goe on boldly, and wee shall not bee suspected." "He saith well," said the King. I went before, he followed, and soe passed through without any hinderance.

[12] I.e., ox-tongues.
[13] The King, Wilmot, Swan, and the two Gounters. Phillips went off to London to arrange for money to be sent to the King in Rouen. Thomas Gounter was dismissed near Stanstead.
[14] Replacing "of."

It was then betweene three and fower of the clock in the afternoone. Wee went on, but had not gone farre but a new terror possessed [15] us: the same soldiers riding after us, as fast as they could. Whereupon the King gave mee a hem. I slackt my pace till they were come up to mee, and by that tyme the souldiers were come, whoe rudely passed by us (beeing in a narrow lane), soe that wee could hardly keepe our [16] sadles for them; but passed by without any further hurt, being some 30 or 40 in number.

When wee were come to Beeding, a little village where I had provided a retreatment for the King (one Mr. Bagshall's house), I was earnest that his Majestie would stay there a whyle, till I had viewed the coast. But my Lord Wilmot would by noe meanes, for feare of those soldiers, but carried the King out of the roade I knowe not whether. Soe wee parted: they where they thought safest, I to Brighthemston, being agreed they should send to mee when fixed anywhere and readie.

Being come to the said Brighthemston, I found all cleere there and the inne (the George) free from all strangers att that tyme. Having taken the best roome in the house and bespoken my supper, as I was entertaining myselfe with a glass [17] of wine, the King, not finding accommodation elsewhere to his mind, was come to the inne. And upp comes myne host (one Smith by name) "More guests," saith he to mee. He brought them up into another roome, I taking noe notice. It was not long, but drawing towards the Kings roome, I heard the Kings voice saying aloud to my Lord Wilmot: "Here, Mr. Barlow, I drinck to you." "I knowe that name," said I to myne hoast, then by mee. "I pray enquire, and whether he was not a major in the Kings army." Which done, hee was found to bee the man whome I expected; and presently invited (as was likely) to the fellowship of a glasse of wine. From that, I proceeded and made a motion to joyne companie and because my chamber was largest, that they would make use of it: which was accepted, and soe wee became one companie againe.

At supper, the King was cheerefull, not shewing the least

[15] The British Museum copy corrects "possessed" to "pursued."
[16] Replacing "you."
[17] Replacing "cupp." This change is also made in the British Museum copy.

signe of feare or apprehension of any daunger, neyther then nor att any tyme during the whole course of this busines. Which is noe small wonder, considering that the very thought of his ennemies, soe great and soe many, soe diligent, and soe much interested in his ruine, was enough, as long as he was within their reach and as it were in the very middest of them, to have daunted the stoutest courage in the world. As if God had opened his eyes, as he did Elisha's servant at his maister's request, and he had seene an heavenly hoast round about him to guard him which to us was invisible, whoe therefore, though much encouraged by his undauntednes and the assurance of soe good and glorious a cause, yet were not without secret terrours within ourselves, and thought every minut a day, a month, till wee should see his sacred person out of their reach.

Supper ended, the King stood his back against the fyer, leaning over a chaire. Up comes mine host (upon some jealousie, I guesse, not any certain knowledge): but up comes he, whoe called himselfe *Gaius,* runs to the King, catcheth his hand; and kissing it, said, "It shall not bee said but I have kissed the best man's hand in England."

He had waited att the table att supper, where the boatemen alsoe sate with us, and were then present. Whether he had seene or heard anything that could give him any occasion of suspicion, I knowe not. In very deede, the King had a hard task, soe to carrie himselfe in all things that he might be in nothing like himselfe, majestie beeing soe naturall unto him, that even when he said nothing, did nothing, his very lookes (if a man observed) were enough to betray him. It was admirable to see how the King (as though he had not beene concerned in these words, which might have sounded in the eares of another man as the sentence of death) turned about in silence, without any alteration of counternance or taking notice of what had beene said.

About a quarter of an hower after, the King went to his chamber, where I followed him, craved his pardon with earnest protestation that I was as innocent, soe altogether ignorant of the cause how this had happened. "Peace, peace, Colonell," said the King, "the fellow knowes mee, and I him. He was one" (whether soe or not, I know not, but soe the King thought att that tyme) "that belonged to the back-staires to my Father. I hope he is an honest fellow."

After this, I began to treat with the boatman (Tettersfeild by name), asking him in what readines he was. He answered hee could not off that night, because, for more securitie, he had brought his vessell into a creeke and the tyde had forsaken it, soe that it was on ground. It is observable that all the whyle the busines had beene in agitation, to this very tyme, the wind had beene contrarie. The King then opening the windowe, tooke notice that the wind was turned, and told the master of the shipp. Whereupon, because of the wind and a cleare night, I offerd 10*li.* more to the man to gett of that night. But that could not bee.

However, wee agreed hee should take in his companie that night. But it was a great busines that wee had in hand; and God would have us to knowe soe, both by the difficulties that offerd themselves, and by his help he afforded to remoove them. When wee thought wee had agreed, the boateman starts back, and saith "Noe," unlesse I would ensure the barke. Argue it wee did with him how unreasonable it was, beeing soe well paid &c., but to noe purpose, soe that I yeelded at last and 200*li.* was his valuation, which was agreed upon. But then, as though he had beene resolved to frustrate all by unreasonable demands, he required my bond. At which, mooved with much indignation, I began to bee as resolute as he, saying, among other thing, there were more boates to bee had besides his; if hee would not, another should, and made as though I would goe to another.

In this contest, the King happily enterposed: "Hee saith right" (saith his Majestie)," a gentlemans word, especially before witnesses, is as good as his bond." At last the man's stomach [18] came downe; and carrie them he would, whatever came of it; and before he would be taken, he would runn his boate under the water. Soe it was agreed that about twoe in the night they should bee aboard.

The boateman in the meanetyme went to provide for necessaries; and I perswaded the King to take some rest. He did, in his cloaths, and my Lord Wilmot with him, till towards twoe of the night. Then I called them up, shewing them how the tyme

[18] I.e., pride, stubbornness.

went by my watch. Horses beeing ledd by the back way towards
the beach, wee came to the boate and found all readie.

Soe I tooke my leave, craving his Majesties pardon if
anything had happened through error, not want of will or
loyaltie. How willingly I would have waited further but for my
family (being many), which would want mee; and I hoped his
Majestie would not, not doubting but in a very little tyme hee
should bee where he would. My only request to his Majestie was
that he would conceale his instruments, wherein their preservation was soe much concerned. His Majestie promist noebody
should knowe. I abided there, keeping the horses in a readines in
case anything unexpected had happened. At 8 of the clock I saw
them on sayle, and it was the afternoone before they were out of
sight. The wind (ô Providence!) held very good till next morning
to ten of the clock; brought them to a place of Normandie called
Fackham, some three miles of *Havre-de-Grace,* 15 October,
Wendsday. They were noe sooner landed but the wind turned and
a violent storme did arise, in soe much that the boateman was
forced to cutt his cable, lost his anchor, to save his boate; for
which hee required of mee 8*li.* and had it. The boate was back
againe at Chichester by Fryday to take his fraught.

I was not gone out of the towne twoe houres but souldiers
came thither to search for a tall black man, 6 foot and 2 inches
high.

> *Unto thee, o God, doe wee give thancks, unto thee*
> *doe wee give thancks, for that thy Name is neere,*
> *thy wondrous workes declare. Great deliverance*
> *giveth he to his King, and sheweth mercy to his*
> *Annointed.*

F I N I S .

EDITORIAL CHANGES IN THE RACTON COPY

At the end of the title, the seventeenth-century editor has added, "as
itt was taken from his mouth by a person of worth a little before he-
died his death" plus seven or eight words that have been rendered

illegible. In the margin below the date, a note in the editor's hand
has also been rendered illegible.

page 147, l. 5, "resolved" replaces "att Salisburie (inspired by God
himself)"; ll. 12–13, "as for . . . the issue" struck out;
ll. 17–19 "the reader. . . . author was" struck out and replaced by "I must shew the reader his ——— patience
with a few circumstances. For." The editor also apparently
meant to excise to "patience" in l. 20.

page 148, l. 15, "and gott . . . sett att" excised; l. 21 "a hundred
pounds" replaced by "the money"; ll. 14–18 "Which
afforded . . . that day" reduced to "a short collation which
was made readie."

page 149, l. 29, "noble Lord" changed to "my lord Wilmot"; ll. 32,
"tooke . . . . following him" replaced by "accordingly
waited onn him"; l. 38 "The noble Lord" changed to
"My Lord."

page 150, l. 9 "had been taken" changed to "Mrs. Hide had taken";
l. 12 "Soe he said . . . resolved" changed to "Soe it was
resolved"; l. 25 "would" changed to "did."

page 151, l. 13, "The noble" changed to "This Noble"; l. 14 "I"
changed to "He"; ll. 23–24, "(without vanity be it spoken)"
excised; l. 32 "of his . . . whoe was" reduced to "of his,
John Day, a trustie man, whoe was."

page 152, ll. 10–18, "As he . . . . came for it" excised; l. 19, both
examples of "wee" changed to "they"; l. 37 "8th" changed
to "9th."

page 153, l. 21, "att such a place" excised; l. 24, "Slowe faire day
there" changed to "faire att Chichester"; l. 26, marginal
note: "30 myles from Chichester, 35 from Mr. Hydes",
"wee" changed to "they"; l. 31, "the way" changed to "his
proceedings"; l. 35, "he" inserted before "borrowed"; l. 36,
"whoe lent . . . he then had" excised.

page 154, l. 12, "Wee" changed to "They"; 19 and 30, "I" changed to
"The Coll."; l. 24, "Wee" changed to "They."

page 155, l. 2, "this 5o*li*. . . . the 6o*li*." changed to "the 6o*li*. to the
merchant and the 5o*li*. to the boateman"; ll. 10–11, "and
one . . . sister" excised; l. 25 "the noble" excised; ll. 22–
24, "would goe . . . expected mee" changed to "did goe
with him. Soe hee tooke leave of Mr. Hyde for that night,
and went to my Lord Willmot was and had earnestly expected him"; l. 36, "att dinner" excised.

page 156, l. 1, "att a haire" excised; l. 16, "he would ride" changed to "rode"; ll. 17 and 30, "wee" changed to "they"; ll. 26–27 "I know . . . wellcome; and" excised.

page 157, l. 7 "him" changed to "them"; l. 8 "us" to "them"; l. 10 "us" changed to "them"; l. 32 "our" changed to "theire"; l. 35, "us" changed to "them."

page 158, l. 4, after "devise" the editor inserts "and therefore they thought itt convenient to continue a way for his leaving the company yt. soe hee might betake himself to his lodgeing, which he effected after the manner of wispering to his Bro: Mr. Simonds, he sd." The necessary excisions have not been made; l. 7 "wee" changed to "they"; l. 8, "our" changed to "their"; l. 24 "us" to "them"; l. 25, "wee" to "they"; l. 27, "mee" to "the Coll."; ll. 22, 25, 30, 37, "Wee" to "They"; ll. 8, 12, 16, "I" to "the Coll."; l. 8 "hee" to "the King."

page 159, l. 3, "us" to "them"; l. 4, "mee" to "the Coll.," "I slackt my" to "He slackt his," l. 5, "mee" to "him"; l. 7, "our" to "theire"; ll. 9, 11, 12, 14, "I" to "he"; l. 14, "they" to "hee"; l. 16, "mee" to "them," l. 17, "the said" excised; l. 19, "my" to "his," l. 20 "myselfe" to "his selfe." l. 22, "and" to "Then"; l. 23, "to mee" excised, l. 24 "I" to "the Coll."; l. 25, "I" to "he," "myne" to "his," "mee" to "him," l. 28, "and" excised; ll. 29, 31, "I" to "hee"; l. 32, "my" to "his"; l. 33 "wee" to "they".

page 160, l. 8, "at his maister's request" excised; l. 10, "us" to "them"; l. 12, "ourselves" to "themselves"; l. 13, "wee" to "they"; l. 16, "mine" to "the"; ll. 17–18, "but up . . . Gaius" excised, "runs" to "& running"; l. 19, "kissing" to "kisseth", "said" to "saying"; l. 22, "us" to "them"; ll. 17, 24, 35, "I" to "the Coll."; l. 36, "I" to "he."

page 161, ll. 13, 14, 17, 18, "wee" to "they"; l. 15, "us" to "them"; l. 18, "I would ensure" changed to "the Coll. would secure"; ll. 3, 11, 18, "I" to "the Coll."; ll. 20, 26, 37, "I" to "hee"; ll. 32, 37, "night" changed to "morning"; l. 35, "and I" changed to "soe he"; l. 23, "my" to "his."

page 162, l. 1, "my" to "his"; l. 6, "mee" to "him." ll. 3, 5, "I" to "the Coll."; l. 6, "mee" to "the Coll."; l. 22, "of Brighthempson" inserted after "towne."

◄Annotated Index ►

ion, formerly Groom of the Bedchamber, who employed John Pope the butler: 54

GIFFARD (Jefford), Charles, of Chillingham, Staffs., catholic, directs the King to Whiteladies, captured but escaped: 40, 42, 78, 80, 81, 86, 87, 88, 91, 101, 114, 116

GIVES (Guise), Mr, of Worcester, a tailor, informs Parliamentary generals of the King's attack at Worcester, hanged next day: 27

GLOUCESTER: 27

GOUNTER (Gunter, Gounther), Col. George (d. 1661?, probably abroad), of Racton, Sussex, royalist; he was with the royal forces during the Civil War and was then made colonel, having been captured at Chichester in 1642 and served in the siege of Arundel Castle in 1643; in September 1651 he was summoned to London and ordered to pay £200 or suffer sequestration of his estate; arranges for the King's escape from Shoreham (Blaauw says the arrangements were made in a little cottage at Portslade). He had two daughters and a son: 7, 14, 66–72, 83, 140–143, 145–164

GOUNTER, Katharine (d. 1684), wife of the above and daughter of Sir Lawrence Hyde of Salisbury; in 1664 she petitioned for relief for herself and her eight children on the score that her husband's estate was heavily indebted because of his help to the King; she was granted a pension of £200: 148, 149, 150–151, 152

GOUNTER, Capt. Thomas, brother of George Gounter, he served on the royalist side in the siege of Arundel Castle and was captured; helps in the arrangements for the King's escape from Shoreham; in 1661 he was made Clerk of the Crown for North Wales and granted a bounty of £100 in 1671: 142, 143, 149, 150–154, 155, 156, 158

HALL, Henry, hostler with whom the King talks at Charmouth: 82, 126

HAMBLEDON (Hammelton, Hamilton), Hants: 68, 83, 143, 156, 157

HAMNET (Hammet), blacksmith at Lyme, raises suspicion about the King: 126

HAMILTON, William, Duke of (1616–51), Secretary of State for Scotland 1640–43, supporter of Charles II, wounded at Worcester and died nine days later: 29

HARRISON, Thomas (1606–60), Parliamentary general and regicide, directs pursuit of the King after Worcester; refused flight or compromise at the Restoration, and executed: 4, 26

HARTLEBURY CASTLE, Worcs.: 87

HAYNES (Heane), Col. James, governor of Weymouth, commander of the Parliamentary forces going to Jersey: 62

HEALE HOUSE (Hele), Wilts., Mary Hyde's residence on the banks of the Avon near Amesbury, where the King stayed before his escape from Shoreham; the house was rebuilt in 1660: 68, 142, 143, 147, 150

JONES, Rice, loyalist landlord of *The George,* Broad Windsor; the King lodges with him: 82, 129

JONES, William, the King's *alias* at Boscobel as a pretended woodsman: 90

JONES, Mr, of Newton Tony, Sussex, a friend of Col. Phillips: 142

KING'S ARMS INN, Salisbury, meeting place for those planning the King's escape: 139

KIRTON, Edward, the Earl of Hertford's steward at Castle Cary, where the King shelters at the manor-house: 82

LAMBERT, John (1619–83), Parliamentary major-general at Worcester and Cromwell's understudy, convicted of treason in 1662 but his life spared: 4, 26

LANE, Athalia (Anson), wife of Col. John Lane: 96

LANE, Jane (*d.* 1689), eldest child of Thomas Lane of Bentley, resided there with her brother, goes with the King (in guise of her servant) from Bentley to Abbots Leigh and Trent, escaped with her brother to France in December, disguised as peasants, and became a member of the court in exile; after the Restoration she was granted a pension of £1000 and married Sir Clement Fisher: 50, 54, 58, 78, 96, 104, 117–119

LANE, Col. John (1609–67), of Bentley, Staffs., Anglican, royalist, Jane Lane's brother; shelters Wilmot and helps the King to escape to the South; escaped to France in December, granted a pension of £500 after the Restoration and a gift of £1000 in 1666; declined a peerage; married Athalia Anson: 50, 96, 104–105, 109–111, 117–119, 121, 122

LANE, Richard, younger brother of the preceding, royalist, captured at Worcester, in 1662 appointed Chief Customer at Plymouth and later Groom of the Chamber: 30, 80

LANE, Thomas, of Bentley, father of Jane Lane: 58

LANE, Withy, second child of the preceding, married John Petre, rides with the King from Bentley: 52, 81

LANGSTONE, Hants: 152

LASCELLES (Lassels), Henry, soldier, cornet under Colonel Lane during the Civil Wars, cousin of Jane Lane and rides with her and the King from Bentley; later sheltered by Anthony Wilkinson, escaped overseas but returned; in 1662 he was dead and his sister Margaret petitioned for the place of Laundress to the Queen: 54–58, 78, 82

LAUDERDALE, John Maitland, 2nd Earl and 1st Duke of (1616–82), Scottish covenanter and statesman, fought for the King at Worcester and made captive, Secretary for Scottish Affairs 1660–80: 30, 38, 81, 101

LESLIE (Leshley), David (*d.* 1682), Scottish major-general, fought for the King at Worcester, captured in Yorkshire and imprisoned until 1660, created Baron Newark in 1661: 30, 40

TUPPON, Thomas, a crew-member on *The Surprise* when the King sailed to France: 83

TURBEVILLE, Henry (d. 1678), Catholic theologian; the King reads one of his books: 121

UPTON, on the Severn just below Worcester: 27

WADE, Margaret, landlady of *The Queen's Arms*, Charmouth: 82

WALKER, William, of Covenbrook, an old gentleman and neighbor of Thomas Whitgreave, formerly a priest who held occasional services for catholics in the Whiteladies area, shelters Wilmot: 103, 104, 113, 117

WARRINGTON, Lancs.: 4, 26

WARNFORD, Hants, the King dines at *The George* there: 83, 156

WESTLY, Rev. Benjamin (d. 1670), puritan parson at Charmouth, great-grandfather of Samuel Wesley, informs on the King to Robert Butler, deprived of his benefice at the Restoration and became an itinerant preacher and doctor: 126

WEYMOUTH, Dorset, the King plans to escape from: 60, 82

WHITELADIES, Salop, half a mile from Boscobel, seat of the Giffards and formerly a Cistercian nunnery, the King shelters there with Humphrey Penderel: 40, 78, 80, 85, 87, 89, 93, 94, 95, 102, 116, 118

WHITGREAVE (Whitgrave), Thomas (1614–1702), of Moseley Hall, Salop, catholic, served on the royalist side in the Civil War under Thomas Giffard, lived at Moseley with his old mother, shelters the King; M. P. in 1656 and 1658, knighted by Cromwell; in 1662 he petitioned for the Receivership of Hearth-Money for Salop and Staffs., and was granted a pension of £300 in 1666: 6, 7, 14, 15, 50, 81, 84, 88, 89, 92, 94, 95, 96, 98, 99, 101–114, 115–122

WIGAN, Lancs.: 87

WIGHT, Isle of: 74

WILDE MONKTON (Wylde), near Lyme, Dorset; the King briefly stays there with John Ellesdon: 128, 133

WILMOT, Henry, Viscount, later 1st Earl of Rochester (1612?–1658), gentleman of the bedchamber, the King's companion in Scotland and during his flight and escape, in England directing royalist conspirators in 1658, died at Sluys: 1, 5, 30, 38, 40, 48, 50, 56–62, 64, 68, 70–74, 78, 79, 82, 83, 87, 88, 94, 96, 102–106, 113, 116, 117, 120–121, 126, 133, 134, 135, 139, 143, 147, 149–162

WINCHESTER, Hants: 156

WINDSOR, Berks.: 52

WINTER, John, of Dirnham, Glos.; shelters Wilmot: 82

WOGAN, Colonel Thomas, royalist, involved in 1651 revolt in South Wales, covered the King's retreat from Worcester: 29

WOLVERHAMPTON, War.: 40, 48, 92, 103, 116, 121

WOOLFE (Wolfe), Francis (1582–1666), of Madeley, catholic, an old gentleman who shelters the King and Richard Penderel in his